Early Literacy Intervention Activities

Research-Based Instructional Strategies That Promote the Development of Reading, Writing, and Spelling Skills Necessary for Later Literacy Achievement

by
Sherrill B. Flora

illustrated by
Julie Anderson
Vanessa Countryman
Ron Kaufmann

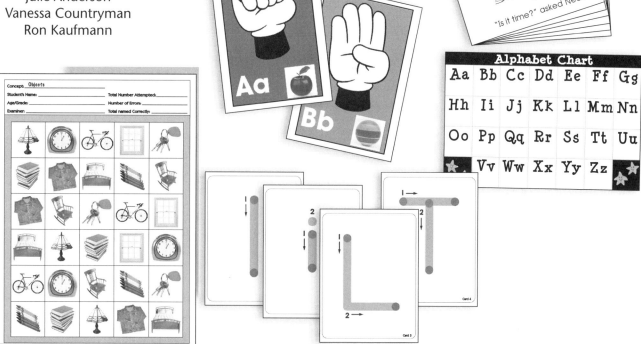

Key Education
An imprint of Carson-Dellosa Publishing LLC
Greensboro, North Carolina

www.keyeducationpublishing.com

CONGRATULATIONS ON YOUR PURCHASE OF A KEY EDUCATION PRODUCT!

The editors at Key Education are former teachers who bring experience, enthusiasm, and quality to each and every product. Thousands of teachers have looked to the staff at Key Education for new and innovative resources to make their work more enjoyable and rewarding. We are committed to developing educational materials that will assist teachers in building a strong and developmentally appropriate curriculum for young children.

PLAN FOR GREAT TEACHING EXPERIENCES WHEN YOU USE EDUCATIONAL MATERIALS FROM KEY EDUCATION PUBLISHING

REFERENCES

Adams, M. 1990. *Beginning to read: Thinking and learning about print*. Cambridge, MA: MIT Press.

Beck, I. L., M. G. McKeown, and L. Kucan. 2002. *Bringing Words to Life: Robust Vocabulary Instruction*. New York: Guilford Press.

Bryant, P. E., M. MacLean, L. L. Bradley, and J. Crossland. 1990. Rhyme and alliteration, phoneme detection, and learning to read. *Developmental Psychology*, 26, 429–438.

Ehri, L. C., S. R. Nunes, D. M. Willows, B. V. Schuster, Z. Yaghoub-Zadeh, and T. Shanahan, 2001. Phonemic awareness instruction helps children learn to read: Evidence from the National Reading Panel's meta-analysis. *Reading Research Quarterly*, 36, 250–287.

Maridaki-Kassotaki, K. 2002. The relation between phonological memory skills and reading ability in Greek-speaking children: Can training of phonological memory contribute to reading development? *European Journal of Psychology of Education*. 17 (1) 63–73, DOI: 10.1007/BF03173205

National Association for the Education of Young Children (NAEYC). 1998. Learning to read and write: Developmentally appropriate practices for young children: A joint position statement of the International Reading Association and the National Association for the Education of Young Children. *Young Children*, 53(4), 30–46.

National Early Literacy Panel. 2009. Developing early literacy: Report of the National Early Literacy Panel. Available online at http://www.nifl.gov/publications/pdf/NELPReport09.pdf

National Institute of Child Health and Human Development. 2000. Report of the National Reading Panel. Teaching children to read: Reports of the subgroups. Available online at http://www.nichd.nih.gov/publications/nrp/report.cfm.

National Reading Panel. 2000. Teaching children to read: An evidence-based assessment of the scientific research literature on reading and its implications for reading instruction. NIH Publication No. 00-4769. Washington, DC: National Institute of Child Health & Human Development, National Institute of Health.

Shaywitz, S. 2003. *Overcoming Dyslexia: A new and complete science-based program for reading problems at any level*. New York: Alfred A. Knopf.

Snow, C., M. Burns, and P. Griffin, ed. 1998. *Preventing reading difficulties in young children*. Washington, D.C.: National Academy Press.

Snyder, L. and D. Downey. 1997. Developmental differences in the relationship between oral language deficits and reading. *Topics in Language Disorders*, 17(3), 27–40.

Stevenson, H. and R. Newman. 1986. Long-term prediction of achievement and attitudes in mathematics and reading. *Child Development*, 57 (3), 646–659.

Torgesen, J. K. 1998. Catch them before they fall. *American Educator*, Spring/Summer, 1–8.

Van Kleeck, A., R. B. Gillam, and L. M. Hoffman. 2006. Training in phonological awareness generalizes to phonological working memory: a preliminary investigation. *The Journal of Speech-Language Pathology and Applied Behavior Analysis*. 1 (3) 228–243 ISSN: 1932-4731

Whitehurst, G. 1992. Dialogic Reading: An Effective Way to Read to Preschoolers. ReadingRockets®. Available online at http://www.readingrockets.org/article 400.

Whitehurst, G., and C. Lonigan. 1998. Child development and emergent literacy. *Child Development*, 69(3), 848–872.

Credits
Author: Sherrill B. Flora
Illustrators: All illustrations are by Julie Anderson, except Vanessa Countryman (Alphabet Mini-Books)
Ron Kaufmann (Sign Language Cards)
Editors: Karen Seberg & Claude Chalk
Cover Design & Production: Annette Hollister-Papp
Page Layout: Key Education Staff
Cover Photographs: © ShutterStock

Key Education
An imprint of Carson-Dellosa Publishing LLC
PO Box 35665
Greensboro, NC 27425 USA
www.keyeducationpublishing.com

TABLE OF CONTENTS

TABLE OF CONTENTS CONT.

Chapter 4: WRITING NAMES & LETTERS & EARLY WRITING EXPERIENCES

Reproducible "Tactile Touch & Trace" Printing Cards

Chapter 5: PHONOLOGICAL MEMORY

Chapter 6: ORAL LANGUAGE

Chapter 7: PRINT AWARENESS

Reproducible "Fold-It" Mini-Books

Chapter 8: TIPS TO ASSIST PARENT INVOLVEMENT

Reproducible Parent Tip Sheets

INTRODUCTION

Early Literacy Research:
The Importance of Language and Literacy Skill Development in Preparing Young Children for Further School Success

Here are some startling research findings:

◆ More than one in three children experience significant difficulties in learning to read.

◆ Only five percent of children learn to read effortlessly.

◆ One in five school age children is a poor reader and remains that way throughout his lifetime.

◆ Of the children identified as having learning disabilities, 80 percent have their primary difficulties in learning to read.

◆ One of the most compelling findings from recent reading research is that children who get off to a poor start in reading rarely catch up.

Here are some hopeful research findings:

◆ The development of early literacy skills through early experiences with books and stories is critically linked to a child's success in learning to read.

◆ There is a strong correlation between the skills with which a child enters school and her later academic performance.

◆ Children can and do learn a great deal about reading during the preschool years before they read independently.

◆ The preschool period is an important time of skill development associated with later reading development.

◆ The years before a child reaches kindergarten are among the most critical in his life to influence learning.

◆ The experience a child has during the first year of schooling has a lasting impact on school performance.

Young children are like sponges. Every day they learn skills that will help them become readers. Early literacy skills begin to develop in infancy and continue to grow through the first five years of life. We now know that a child's likelihood for success in the first grade depends on how much she has learned about reading before entering kindergarten. A child's early experiences with books and language will build the foundation for further success in learning to read.

The National Early Literacy Panel (NELP) was appointed in 2002 and given the enormous task of examining a wealth of early literacy research. Their goal was then to identify the interventions, parenting activities, and instructional practices that would promote the development of early literacy skills in young children. The panel first set out to establish which early skills could be identified to be the precursors of later literacy achievement.

The panel's findings suggest that the strongest predictors of literacy outcomes are:

- ◆ **Alphabet Knowledge:** knowledge of the names and sounds associated with printed letters
- ◆ **Phonological Awareness:** the ability to detect, manipulate, or analyze the auditory aspects of spoken language, including the ability to distinguish or segment words, syllables, or phonemes, independent of meaning
- ◆ **Writing & Writing Name:** the ability to write letters in isolation or to write one's own name
- ◆ **Rapid Automatic Naming:** the ability to rapidly name a sequence of randomly repeating pictures of objects, colors, letters, or digits
- ◆ **Phonological Memory:** the ability to remember spoken information for a short period of time

Some of the next strongest predictors of literacy outcomes are:

- ◆ **Print Concepts and Print Awareness:** the ability to understand a book including right side up, front and back, turning pages, and return sweep and recognizing the nature and uses of print in the environment
- ◆ **Oral Language:** the ability to produce (expressive) or comprehend (receptive) spoken language, including vocabulary and grammar
- ◆ **Visual Processing:** the ability to match or discriminate visually presented symbols

The goal of *Early Literacy Intervention Strategies* is to provide preschool and kindergarten teachers with highly-engaging, research-based intervention strategies, teaching suggestions, activities, and games for helping young children build a foundation of early literacy skills that will assist them in becoming lifelong successful readers.

Effective Teaching Intervention Strategy:
High Quality Literacy Instruction in Preschool and Kindergarten

A review of current research has shown that effective literacy instruction is crucial and that there are specific identifiable characteristics of effective literacy teachers (Williams & Baumann, 2008).

1. An effective teacher will have **high expectations** for her students and understands that students need a **social learning environment** that supports discussions and cooperative learning.

2. An effective teacher knows that **small-group learning is crucial** and large-group lessons are kept to a minimum. One-to-one time, independent activities, learning centers, and projects are incorporated into the literacy curriculum.

3. An effective teacher understands that a classroom of students with diverse learning styles will require a **variety of strategies**. A teacher needs to be **well-versed in a multitude of methods and techniques** and is able to put them into practice in the classroom.

4. An effective teacher will also **use a large variety of materials to enhance the various teaching methods**. A wealth of literature and varied genres, authentic texts, newspapers, magazines, and other materials can be employed to encourage reading across all content areas.

5. An effective teacher will **consistently assess the students' skills using a variety of evaluation techniques** (formal and informal) and then **differentiate instruction** according to the needs of the students.

6. An effective teacher will **create a positive learning environment** where students are praised and the teacher is **sensitive, empathetic, enthusiastic, compassionate**, and **willing to share her own stories and interests** through exciting and motivating lessons.

Chapter 1
ALPHABET KNOWLEDGE

Why Teach Alphabet Knowledge?

"Knowledge of the alphabet at school entry is one of the single best predictors of eventual reading achievement." (Adams, 1990; Stevenson & Newman, 1986)

Alphabet knowledge may sound like a simple concept, but it is an extremely important part of a young child's literacy development. It refers to the child's ability to:

- ◆ identify letters by shape
- ◆ identify letters by name
- ◆ identify letters by sound
- ◆ print letters
- ◆ rapidly name letters in a random sequence

Children cannot learn to read words without a solid knowledge of the alphabet. Children beginning first grade who cannot quickly say and write the alphabet will need a great deal of organized practice in order for them to identify, name, and write letters.

What Are Some Effective Ways to Teach Alphabet Knowledge?

All children enter school with a wide range of skills when it comes to alphabet knowledge. Some fortunate children come from families that read together, have fun reciting the alphabet, sing alphabet songs, and play games that encourage early literacy. Other children come from families where these types of early literacy experiences are not a part of their daily lives.

An effective teacher understands that the children in her classroom will have a wide variety of skills and abilities. She will assess each child's alphabet knowledge and then plan effective teaching strategies designed to meet the individual needs of her students. The following are some general guidelines for teaching alphabet knowledge:

- ◆ Provide a variety of multisensory activities that will help children learn to identify and name both upper- and lowercase letters.

- ◆ Use games, songs, rhymes, and chants to help children learn to name letters quickly.

- ◆ Provide fine motor and various writing experiences for children to practice making the shapes of letters.

- ◆ Fill a classroom library with alphabet books and read aloud books that will help children explore and experiment with language.

ALPHABET KNOWLEDGE:
MULTISENSORY INTERVENTION STRATEGIES

Multisensory Activities Are Crucial

Howard Gardner's theory of multiple intelligences, developed in 1983, brought to the attention of educators the theory that everyone has different styles of learning. People have unique strengths, and they perceive, organize, conceptualize, and recall information in varying ways.

Using a multisensory approach to teach alphabet knowledge—combining visual, auditory, and tactile experiences—will simultaneously provide all children with the opportunity to utilize their most dominant learning styles. This instructional method offers children the most comprehensive learning experience.

Multisensory activities that involve seeing, speaking, listening, and touching are designed to help children learn faster—not only children who are struggling—but all of the children in your classroom.

Introduce Alphabet Letters in a Variety of Ways

1. **Introduce the name of the letter.** Say the letter name and have children repeat it.

2. **Introduce the way the letter looks.** Show children a large version of the letter. Talk about what the letter looks like. Does it have a circle? A tall straight line? A tail that goes below the line? Does it remind them of anything? A *b* looks like a ball and a bat. A *j* looks like a fishing hook. An *A* could be described as a tent. A *U* looks like a smile.

3. **Have children listen to the sound the letter makes.** Say the letter sound for the children and then have them repeat the sound back to you.

4. **Develop an awareness of how the letter feels in the mouth.** After children have heard the sound the letter makes, have them make the sound while they are looking in a mirror. Tell them to look at how their tongues and lips move and the position of their teeth. Have them put their hands in front of their mouths to see if they can feel the sound (e.g., /b/ and/t/ produce a breath). Children may also want to touch their lips or throat to feel letter vibrations (e.g., /m/ and /z/). Watching themselves in a mirror as they make letter sounds will help them remember the sounds.

5. **Create the letter with large muscle movement.** Have children "draw" the letter in the air or use a paintbrush and water on a chalkboard. The large muscle movement will also help children remember the letter shapes and names.

6. **Use a word that is associated with the letter.** Add the new letter to an alphabet wall and post a picture to help children associate the letter with the letter sound. A picture of a beach ball will help children remember the letter *b*.

7. **Look at the way the letter looks within a word.** Add to the alphabet wall several words—or names of the children—that contain that particular letter. This visual cue serves as another memory tool.

ALPHABET KNOWLEDGE: SHARED READING CHARTS

Large Classroom Alphabet Chart

Large alphabet-chart posters are made by a variety of publishers, or you may simply create your own. Laminate the chart so that it is durable and can be used with dry erase markers for write on/wipe off activities. Display the chart for shared group readings; you or a child should point to each letter (or the picture clue) as it is read. For fun, use different voices—loud, soft, silly, etc.—as you chant the alphabet together.

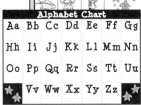

My Own Alphabet Charts

Provide each child with an individual alphabet chart for shared group reading activities. The children can touch each letter as they say the letter's name. On pages 10 and 11, you will find four different alphabet charts—each chart was created in a different font. This helps children learn that letters appear in a variety of styles. Copy a chart for each child and laminate for durability. After a child is secure with the letter style of one alphabet chart, exchange it for one with another font.

Tabletop or Desktop Alphabet Lines

Copy the alphabet chart at the bottom of the page for each child. Laminate the charts and tape one at the place where each child sits. The children can use these desktop alphabet lines as a reference tool.

Helpful Hint: Eye-Level Chalkboard Alphabet Lines

It is helpful to display the large, classroom alphabet line at the children's eye level. Often, teachers place alphabet lines up high over the chalkboard where they are difficult for young children to actually use as a reference tool.

Alphabet Walls

Acquaint children with the alphabet wall on the first day of school and use it daily. Place words and pictures under each letter as you introduce the individual letters. Make sure that the words you choose are meaningful to the children—use their names (with a photo of each child), thematic words, and words chosen by the children. As space fills up, remove older words and add new ones. This will keep the wall fresh and interesting. Begin with uppercase letters and add lowercase letters as they are introduced. Make sure to use a font that is large enough to be easily read by the children and place letters at their eye level.

Tabletop or Desktop Alphabet Lines—Display whole or fold in half to show just the upper- or lowercase letters.

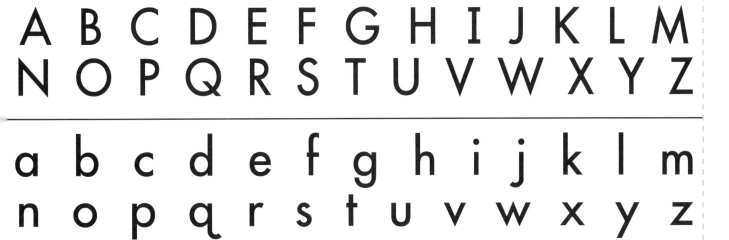

Alphabet Chart

Aa	Bb	Cc	Dd	Ee	Ff	Gg
Hh	Ii	Jj	Kk	Ll	Mm	Nn
Oo	Pp	Qq	Rr	Ss	Tt	Uu
	Vv	Ww	Xx	Yy	Zz	

Directions are found on page 9.

Alphabet Chart

Aa	Bb	Cc	Dd	Ee	Ff	Gg
Hh	Ii	Jj	Kk	Ll	Mm	Nn
Oo	Pp	Qq	Rr	Ss	Tt	Uu
	Vv	Ww	Xx	Yy	Zz	

Alphabet Chart

Aa	Bb	Cc	Dd	Ee	Ff	Gg
Hh	Ii	Jj	Kk	Ll	Mm	Nn
Oo	Pp	Qq	Rr	Ss	Tt	Uu
	Vv	Ww	Xx	Yy	Zz	

Directions are found on page 9.

Alphabet Chart

Aa	Bb	Cc	Dd	Ee	Ff	Gg
Hh	Ii	Jj	Kk	Ll	Mm	Nn
Oo	Pp	Qq	Rr	Ss	Tt	Uu
	Vv	Ww	Xx	Yy	Zz	

♪ ALPHABET KNOWLEDGE: SING THE ALPHABET ♪

The "Alphabet Song" is probably the most commonly used tool to help teach the names of the letters. Young children simply sing along while they unknowingly acquire an important prereading skill. The importance of this step cannot be overlooked because several letters' names relate closely to the speech sounds associated with them. Automatic recall of letter names also makes it easier for the child to learn and label the letter shapes in future lessons.

Favorite Recordings of Alphabet Songs

Find traditional or alternative versions of the "Alphabet Song" and have children sing along with the music. Introduce each musical selection to the class before placing it in the literacy or music center. If there is a companion book, read it aloud without interruptions so that your students may enjoy the story. Reread the book at another time to discuss any new vocabulary words that are used. Keep the tone of the discussions playful.

Missing Alphabet Letters

When you sing the alphabet song for the class, occasionally leave out two or three letters and let children discover the mistakes. If you would like this challenge to be gamelike, have the children who identify the missing letters form a group and sing the song again. Let the other students judge whether the lyrics were sung correctly. Conclude this activity by reading aloud the book *Alphabet Mystery* by Audrey Wood (Blue Sky Press, 2003) and find out what happens when Little *x* is missing.

Duplicate one for each child to use as the class sings together.

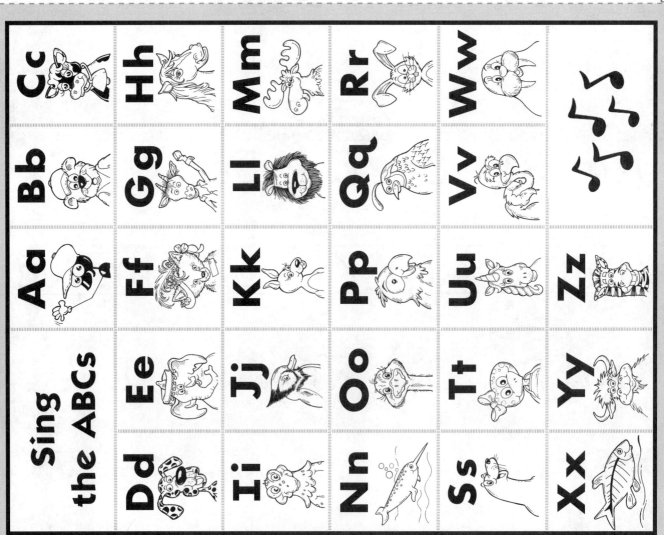

ALPHABET BOOK LIST & ACTIVITIES

A Is for Animals by David Pelham (Little Simon, 2001)

A My Name Is Alice by Jane Bayer (Puffin, 1992)

The ABC Bunny by Wanda Gag (University of Minnesota Press, 2004)

ABC I Like Me! by Nancy Carlson (Puffin, 1999)

Alison's Zinnia by Anita Lobel (Greenwillow, 1996)

Alphabatics by Suse MacDonald (Aladdin, 1992)

Alphabet Adventure by Audrey Wood (Blue Sky Press, 2001)

Alphabet Mystery by Audrey Wood (Blue Sky Press, 2003)

Alphabet Rescue by Audrey Wood (Blue Sky Press, 2006)

The Alphabet Tree by Leo Lionni (Knopf Books for Young Readers, 2004)

Alphabet under Construction by Denise Fleming (Henry Holt, 2006)

AlphaOops! The Day Z Went First by Alethea Kontis (Candlewick, 2006)

The Alphazeds by Shirley Glaser (Miramax, 2003)

Chicka Chicka Boom Boom by Bill Martin Jr. and John Archambault (Beach Lane Books, 2009)

The Circus Alphabet by Linda Bronson (Henry Holt, 2001)

City Seen from A to Z by Rachel Isadora (William Morrow, 1992)

Curious George Learns the Alphabet by H. A. Rey (Houghton Mifflin, 1993)

Dr. Seuss's ABC: An Amazing Alphabet Book! by Theodor Geisel (Random House, 1996)

Eating the Alphabet: Fruits & Vegetables from A to Z by Lois Ehlert (Harcourt, 1996)

Eric Carle's ABC by Eric Carle (Grosset & Dunlap, 2007)

Firefighters A to Z by Chris L. Demarest (McElderry, 2000)

Kindergarten ABC by Jacqueline Rogers (Scholastic, 2002)

Little Monster's Alphabet Book by Mercer Mayer (Golden Press, 1978)

Maisy's ABC by Lucy Cousins (Walker Books, LTD> 2008)

Matthew A.B.C. by Peter Catalanotto (Atheneum, 2002)

Miss Spider's ABC by David Kirk (Scholastic, 1998)

The Ocean Alphabet Book by Jerry Pallotta (Charlesbridge, 1986)

Q Is for Duck: An Alphabet Guessing Game by Mary Elting and Michael Folsom (Clarion, 2005)

Shiver Me Letters: A Pirate ABC by June Sobel (Sandpiper, 2009)

Sleepy Little Alphabet: A Bedtime Tale from Alphabet Town by Judy Sierra (Knopf, 209)

26 Letters and 99 Cents by Tana Hoban (Greenwillow, 1995)

Z Goes Home by Jon Agee (Hyperion Books for Children, 2003)

Collect a Variety of Alphabet Books

Use alphabet books for reading aloud and shared reading activities. Read a book daily, especially during the first of the year.

ABC Book Reading Suggestions:

◆ Discuss the pattern of the book. For example, point out that each page may represent one alphabet letter, so all of the words on the page may begin with that letter or all the pictures may begin with that letter's sound.

◆ After children are familiar with the story, cover the letters with self-stick notes and ask the children to predict what letter they think is behind each note.

◆ To make learning the letters in the story more meaningful, relate the letter on each page to things the children are familiar with: their names, objects in your classroom, letters already displayed on the room's letter or word wall, and so on.

Make Your Own ABC Books

Alphabet knowledge can be strengthened when children make their own ABC books. You may choose to make a large classroom book as a group project, have the children make their own individual books, or both!

Individual Book: Complete an 8.5" x 11" page each time a letter is introduced. Let children collect pictures from magazines, photographs, and artwork. Write or help each child to write the upper- and lowercase letters on each page. Then, the child may glue the cut out pictures or draw things that represent the letter. Keep the pages in a folder or three-ring binder so that they are in order and can easily be added to.

Class book: Each child will make one or two pages, depending your class's size. Allow several days for this project. Using poster board or 11" x 17" paper, create pages as described above. Bind the pages together as a big book with yarn or rings.

ALPHABET KNOWLEDGE:
MAKE LETTERS MEANINGFUL—NAMES

Young children are eager to learn about the letters in their first and last names and how to write them. And, many young children are also fascinated with the written names of their classmates. Here are a few activity ideas to help children make meaningful connections with letters in their names.

Names and Photographs Schoolhouse

On a bulletin board or large chart, make a cutout of a schoolhouse large enough to have a window for each child. Take a photograph of each child and attach it to an index card (*see illustration*). On the other side of the card print the child's name. Place a brad above each window section and a paper clip on the top of each index card.

(front of card) *(back of card)*

Hang an index card in each "window" on the schoolhouse with the name side showing. Invite children to find their names and turn the cards around so that their photos show. Repeat the activity without rearranging the cards. As the children become more secure in identifying their printed names, rearrange the cards so that the activity becomes more challenging.

Crack the Egg

On slips of paper, print the names of your students. Put each prepared piece of paper into a colorful plastic egg. Place the eggs in a basket. Pair the children and have them stand behind a special starting line. Let each pair hop (march, skip, leap, stomp, etc.) to the basket, select their eggs, and then hop back to the start. After every child has retrieved an egg from the basket, it's time to crack them open. Have the children figure out the names and then deliver the eggs to the owners, who then put them back in the basket. Play the game again.

Our Classroom Name Book

This book will become a classroom treasure to be enjoyed all year long. It will also help the children learn to read each other's names. Take a photograph of each child and tape it on a piece of 8.5" x 11" card stock. Print the child's name above the photo. Let the children decorate their pages. Place each finished page in a sheet protector. (The book will get a lot of wear and tear throughout the year.) Then, tape another piece of card stock on the sheet protector over the photograph to cover it like a flap. As children "read" the name on each page, they can lift up the flap to discover the photograph.

Play Traditional Games

It is easy to create traditional games such as Bingo, Lotto, and Memory Match using letters from the names of the children in your class.

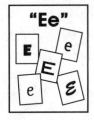

Name Puzzles and Alphabet Wall

Print each child's name on a sentence strip. Let the children cut apart the letters and keep them in envelopes. Invite them to put together and take apart their names.

Children will also enjoy cutting apart their names and then gluing each letter on the correct page on the letter wall. As the children cut apart the letters, ask them to tell you the letter name before they glue it on the letter wall.

ALPHABET KNOWLEDGE:
MAKE LETTERS MEANINGFUL—NAMES

Sorting Using Letters in Names

They are many fun sorting games children can play using their names, such as:

1. Sort names by the first letter.
2. Sort names by the last letter.
3. Sort names that have the same number of letters.
4. Sort names that have the same letter clusters.
5. Sort names by those that have "tall" letters, letters with "tails," letters with "dots," or letters with "circles."

A Book about Me

Have the children make books about themselves. They can include pages about their families, pets, all of their likes and dislikes, and their favorite things. On each page, use the child's name in a simple sentence, such as, "This book is about **Katie**. **Katie** has a cat. **Katie's** favorite color is blue. **Katie** has a little sister. **Katie** likes to eat ice cream." As these books become favorites, children will learn to recognize other words besides their names.

Whose Name Has the Letter "_____" in It?

Record the first names of your students on sentence strips or on copies of the pattern shown below. It is helpful to include a picture along with each name. Later, remove the pictures when the students are becoming very familiar with their classmates' names. Play games with the prepared materials by asking various questions that are related to the letters in the names.

Aa Bb Cc Dd Ee Ff Gg Hh Ii Jj Kk Ll Mm

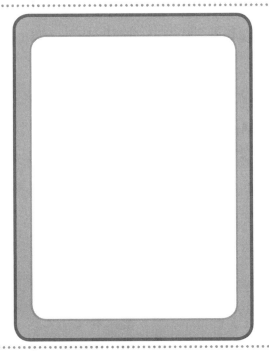

My name is . . .

Nn Oo Pp Qq Rr Ss Tt Uu Vv Ww Xx Yy Zz

ALPHABET KNOWLEDGE: LETTER SORTS

Letter sorting activities allow children the opportunity to explore and discover things about letters. These activities help them gain in the development of automaticity and independent letter recognition.

Lots and Lots of Alphabet Letter Fonts

Students not only have to learn to identify letters typeset in books but also handwritten letters—which is really 104 letters in total! To draw attention to this diversity in letter shapes, create an alphabet letter wall that features lots of different examples for each letter form. Children can help you with this collection by looking for letter shapes in magazines, newspapers, computer printouts, and handwritten notes. Encourage children to ask their parents to write the alphabet on index cards and add those writing samples to the display. They will be amazed to see how different the letter shapes may look for the same alphabet letter!

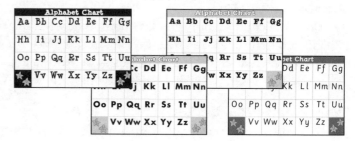

Variation: Cut apart the letters found on the reproducible Alphabet Charts on pages 10 and 11. (Each chart was created using a different font.) The children can make their own individual alphabet letter wall pages or alphabet books using the letters from these charts.

What Do the Letters Have in Common?

It is also meaningful for children to sort letters by attributes that the letters have in common. For example, letters can be sorted according to: tall letters (e.g., *l, h, f*), letters with slanted lines (e.g., *A, V, W*) letters that have tails (e.g., *g, q, p*), letters with circles (e.g., *O, Q, o*), letters with smiles (e.g., *u, j, U*), and letters with frowns (e.g., *n, m, h*).

As the children gain knowledge (especially in later kindergarten) the letters can be sorted by consonants and vowels. These sorting activities help children focus on what each letter really looks like.

Alphabet Animal Boxes

What you need: 26 small clean milk cartons, the reproducible "Sing the ABCs Chart" (page 12), contact paper or wrapping paper, glue, and scissors.

What you do: Enlarge the chart and cut out each letter and animal face section on the lines. Cover each small milk carton with contact paper or wrapping paper. Glue a letter and its animal face onto each milk carton. Cut a hole in the carton above the animal face. **(The animals featured on the chart are A–ant, B–bear, C–cow, D–dog, E–elephant, F–fox, G–goat, H–horse, I–iguana, J–jay, K–kangaroo, L–lion, M–moose, N–Narwhal, O–ostrich, P–parrot, Q–quail, R–rabbit, S–seal, T–turtle, U–unicorn, V–vulture, W–walrus, X–X-ray fish, Y–yak, Z–zebra.)** The children can sort letters (magnetic letters, foam letters, letters cut from magazines and newspapers, etc.) into each milk carton. Later, when letter sounds are introduced, children can sort pictures of objects whose names begin with the letters into the animal letter cartons.

Sorting Alphabet Cereal

Place small paper plates on a table. Label each plate with a letter. Give each child a small cup of letter-shaped cereal pieces or letter-shaped dried macaroni. The children can sort the letter shapes onto the matching letter plates.

ALPHABET KNOWLEDGE: LETTER SORTS

Alphabet Clothespin Wheel Games

What you need: sturdy paper plates, spring-type clothespins, and markers.

Matching Letters Wheel: Print letters around the edge of a paper plate. Print one alphabet letter on the end of each clothespin. The children can match the letter on the clothespin to the corresponding letter on the paper plate and then clip the clothespin by the correct letter.

Clothespin Wheel Bingo: Write 8 to 10 letters around the edge of a paper plate; make a plate for each child in the class. Give each child 8 to 10 unlabeled clothespins. Hold up a letter. If a child has that letter on her paper plate, she should clip a clothespin by the letter (*see illustration*). The first child to have a clothespin by every letter on his plate is the winner.

Alphabet Clothespin Can Games

You can play the same letter sorting games as above by using a can or an empty cylindrical oatmeal box and clothespins (*see illustration*).

Sorting the "Easy-to-Reverse" Letters

I experienced success when I would have my struggling students sort the "easy-to-reverse" letters a few at a time. It is common for children, even those in second grade, to still make occasional reversals. Here are some suggestions to help students recognize these difficult to identify letters.

---

b and d

1. When you need to remember which way "**b**" faces and which way "**d**" faces, just think about the two letters as "good friends." Say the first four letters of the alphabet: a, **b**, c, **d**; "**b**" comes first and faces "**d**."

3. "**b**" looks like a **bat** and a **ball**. "**d**" looks like a **ball** and a **bat**.

2. Place your hands palms down on a table. Spread your pointer fingers and thumbs far apart. Visualize a "**b**" fitting inside your left hand. Visualize a "**d**" fitting inside your right hand.

4. Draw a pair of glasses for each child. Say, "Look at the glasses. Can you see the "**b**" and the "**d**"? Color the "**b**" side of the glasses red. Color the "**d**" side of the glasses blue.

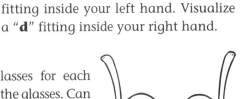

---

p and q

1. **Porcupine** begins with "**p**." The porcupine is looking for its quills.

Quills begins with "**q**." The quills protect the porcupine.

2. Remember when you learned that "**b**" faces "**d**"—well, "**p**" faces "**q**" too! Just say the alphabet, and you will see that "**p**" comes before "**q**."

3. Place your hands palms up and have your little fingers touching. Visualize the "**p**" hanging over the end of your left thumb. Now, visualize a "**q**" hanging over your right thumb.

M and W

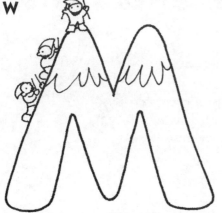

The **M**en are **M**arching up
and down the **M**ountain.

"**W**" is for **W**orm. I **W**onder
Why a **W**orm **W**iggles?

n and u

"**n**" looks like a frow**n**.

"**n**" looks like a **n**ose.

"**u**" looks like a smile.

"**U**" looks like a c**U**p.

letter Ss

Start by drawing a "C" and
then go back the other **W**ay!

"**S**" is for a
Slithering **S**nake
who says,
"**S S S S S S.**"

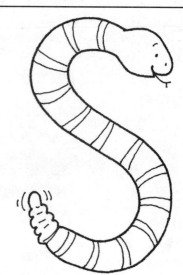

ALPHABET KNOWLEDGE: TACTILE ACTIVITIES

Make Tactile Alphabet Cards

Copy the alphabet letter cards (pages 125–137) on card stock. Cut them out along the dashed lines. Place a thin coat of white glue along each letter and then sprinkle it with sand or glitter. When the cards have dried, children can trace over each letter and feel its shape. This multisensory technique will help children remember the name of the letter as they see the letter, touch the letter, and say the name of the letter out loud.

Write Letters with a Variety of Materials

Children love to explore letters using a variety of tactile materials. Here are some ideas for materials to use and recipes to try for more tactile experiences.

Dry materials: Fill a cookie sheet or shallow cake pan with flour, sand, rice, sugar, salt, or glitter and let children experiment with creating letters and feeling the shapes as they draw.

Moist or wet materials: On a tabletop covered with a plastic tablecloth, the children can make letters with their fingers using finger paint, shaving cream, hair gel, liquid soap, or prepared instant pudding. Children will also enjoy painting letters on a chalkboard with a paintbrush and water.

Make Your Own Puffy Paint

What you need: flour, salt, liquid tempera paint, heavy card stock or cardboard, empty squeeze bottles (with narrow nozzles), mixing bowls, and paper towels.

What you do: Mix equal parts of flour, salt, and water together in a bowl. Add tempera paint for color. Mix well and pour into a squeeze bottle that has a narrow nozzle. Squeeze the puffy paint onto cardboard or heavy card stock. The mixture will harden as it dries.

No-Cook Baker's Clay

What you need: 4 cups (946 ml) flour, 1 cup (236 ml) salt, 1 teaspoon (5 ml) powered alum, 2 cups (473 ml) water, and food coloring.

What you do: Mix the flour, salt, and powdered alum together. Slowly mix the water into the flour mixture. *(Special Tip:* For even distribution of color, add the food coloring to the water before the water is mixed with the other ingredients.) Knead for several minutes. You may wish to divide the dough into smaller balls and then add a different food coloring to each section of dough. Store in airtight containers. Use alphabet letter cookie cutters or create your own letter shapes. Carefully place letters on an ungreased cookie sheet and bake for 30 minutes in a 250° oven. Turn the letters over and bake another 30 minutes.

Make Your Own Stamps

This is an inexpensive way to create stamps for young children. Save old wooden blocks, which are easy for small hands to hold and control. Cut out alphabet letters (flip over stencils if needed to reverse the letters before tracing) from self-adhesive shoe liners; heavy, self-adhesive mounting tape; or craft foam. Craft foam will have to be glued to the surface of the wooden block. Peal off the backing paper from the shoe liners or self-adhesive mounting tape and simply stick the cutout letter to the wooden block.

Use commercially purchased washable stamping ink pads with the block stamps. Or, place a folded paper towel in an aluminum pie pan to act as a stamping pad and soak it with tempera paint.

ALPHABET KNOWLEDGE: LEARNING GAMES

"I Spy" Letters in the Room

Pair children and have them search for designated letters on books in the library corner; on signs in the learning centers; and on charts, cubbies, lockers, and so on. Direct them to search everywhere except your word wall if you have one. Have them make a tally mark on a piece of paper each time they find one of the letters.

Wikki Stix® Fun

On chart paper, write a nursery rhyme or short poem that features letters that you may be focusing on with the students. Have them come up and make Wikki Stix® circles around the featured letters. This is also a fun, independent activity when a small amount of text is provided on an 8.5" x 11" piece of paper.

What Letter Is Missing?

Increase children's visual memory of alphabet letters by playing a "What Letter Is Missing?" game. Place four to five alphabet cards along the chalkboard ledge. Have the children name the letters on the cards. Then, ask children to close their eyes while you remove one of the cards. Tell them to open their eyes and look at the cards. Then, say, "What card is missing?" The child who guesses correctly can be next to remove a card.

Giant Alphabet Dice

Use clean milk cartons (or square boxes if you can find them.) You will need two milk cartons to make one alphabet die. Cut the milk cartons in half and then push one bottom half into the other bottom half to form a solid cube. Cover the cube in colored contact paper. Print an alphabet letter on each side of the cube. You may wish to make five cubes so that all of the alphabet letters can be represented. Have children take turns tossing the cubes and calling out the letter they see on the top.

Letter Murals

On a large piece of chart paper, print the letter that you wish to target. Give children old magazines, newspapers, and catalogs and ask them to find the letter in as many places as they can. Encourage them to look for the letter in different sizes, colors, and fonts. The children should cut out the letters and glue them onto the chart paper.

Match Uppercase and Lowercase Magnetic Letters

Let the children match uppercase and lowercase magnetic letters. Small cookie sheets work well in an alphabet learning center. Or, use the side of a metal file cabinet. Children will enjoy sitting beside the cabinet to match the letters.

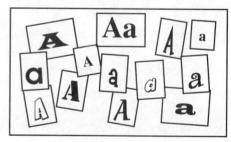

Alphabet Concentration

Choose 8 to 12 letters and create a set of letter cards, making two cards for each letter. Have children lay the cards facedown and take turns picking up two cards at a time. If the letters on the cards match, the child keeps them and takes another turn. The game is over when all of the cards have been chosen.

Variation: The game can be played by matching uppercase to uppercase letters, matching lowercase to lowercase letters, or by matching uppercase to lowercase letters.

ALPHABET KNOWLEDGE: GROSS MOTOR ACTIVITIES

Hopscotch Games

You will need a discarded plastic window shade, a vinyl tablecloth, or a plastic shower curtain. Cut the plastic into strips that can be taped together to make a long indoor "sidewalk." Draw a hopscotch grid or simply divide the sidewalk into squares.

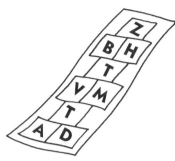

Print a different alphabet letter in each section. Invite children to take turns tossing beanbags onto the sidewalk and then naming the letter written in the section where the beanbag landed.

Alphabet Baseball

This traditional game is great fun and can really help children learn to recognize and identify letters. First, prepare 26 flash cards, one for each alphabet letter. Make another set of cards with the words *single, double, triple, homerun,* and *out*. Each word should appear on several cards, with more *single* and *out* cards than *homerun* cards. Shuffle both sets of cards. Then, use masking tape to create a baseball diamond—including the bases and running lines—in your classroom or go outside and designate an area as the baseball field. The pitcher stands on the pitcher's mound holding the alphabet letter flash cards. The pitcher shows the batter a letter card. If the batter names the letter correctly, he draws a word card and goes to that base, or he may be out!

Play the game with real baseball rules. A team loses the batting position when there are three outs. Players advance to the next base with each hit just like in a baseball game.

Follow the ABC Path

Cut out stones from gray or brown construction paper and print an alphabet letter on each stone. Laminate the stones for durability. Early in the year tape them on the floor of your classroom in alphabetical sequence. A child can say or sing the alphabet song while walking along the letter path.

As the year progresses, scramble the letters so that children must search for each letter in order to step on the letters alphabetically. For a challenge, children can also walk along the scrambled alphabet path and identify each letter as they step on it.

Z, You Can't Catch Me!

Have the children form a circle and sit down with crossed legs. Explain to the class that the game's rules are similar to Duck, Duck, Goose or Duck, Duck, Grey Duck. Select one child to be "It." The chosen child walks around the circle, lightly tapping the top of each player's head while simultaneously saying a letter of the alphabet (without repeating any letters). At anytime, "It" can call out the letter Z. The player tapped on Z jumps up to chase "It" around the circle. If "It" avoids being tagged by player Z, "It" sits down in player Z's spot. Player Z then becomes "It" and the game continues in the same manner.

Flashlight Letters

Print large alphabet letters on the chalkboard. Let children take turns tracing over the letters with a flashlight as they say the name of each letter. The large motor movement will help children better remember the letters' shapes and names.

- Alphabet attributes corner
- Alphabet books (commercial or teacher created)
- Alphabet charts (a variety)
- Alphabet cookie cutters
- Alphabet lotto games
- Alphabet placemats
- Alphabet rugs
- Alphabet sticker books for each child
- Blocks
- Board games
- Butcher paper
- Chalkboards
- Daily writing record for each child
- Desktop alphabet charts
- Foam letters
- Letter cards
- Letter tiles
- Letter walls
- Magna Doodle® drawing toys
- Magnetic boards or surfaces for sorting
- Magnetic letters
- Matching games
- Names chart
- Names corner with students' names and pictures
- Paintbrushes and water
- Play dough or clay
- Pocket charts and/or shoe bags
- Puzzles
- Salt and sand trays
- Sandpaper letters
- Stamps
- Stencils
- Whiteboards and markers
- Wikki Stix®
- Word wall pointers of assorted sizes and types such as bubble wands, wooden spoons, etc.

ALPHABET KNOWLEDGE: ALPHABET MINI-BOOKS

How to Prepare and Use the Alphabet Mini-Books—Pages 33–63

There are 31 reproducible storybooks consisting of 21 beginning consonant sound stories, 5 short vowel sound stories, and 5 long vowel sound stories.

How to Prepare: Reproduce a storybook for each child. Color, cut out along the dotted lines, and staple the pages in numerical order.

How to Use: Read the story while the children listen carefully. Have them follow along and turn the pages as directed. Next, begin the story again. As you read each line, invite children to "read" the line after you. Before long the children will become familiar with the story. Ask them if they hear any similar sounds. Can they name words that have the same sound? Later, have the children go through the mini-book and circle the designated letters with a crayon.

The children in your classroom will be thrilled when they are allowed to keep and take home these storybooks. They will be excited to share stories they have learned to read at school. What an easy and inexpensive way to get reading materials into the hands of children and their families. Watch the eyes of the children light up as they get to call each new story their own!

ALPHABET KNOWLEDGE: ASSESSMENT DIRECTIONS

Consistent assessment and the recording of progress is crucial to individualizing education and ensuring that students are learning. Two reproducible checklists are available for your record keeping—an Uppercase Letter Identification Checklist (page 24) and a Lowercase Letter Identification Checklist (page 25).

The student will be asked to perform the following on both of the checklists:

1. **Letters in ABC order:** Have the child look at the complete alphabet in Box 1 on page 24 or 25 and touch and read the letters in alphabetical order.

    A B C D E F G H I J K L M N O P Q R S T U V W X Y Z (or)
    a b c d e f g h i j k l m n o p q r s t u v w x y z

2. **Small set of letters in random order:** Scatter on a table surface a set of selected letter cards, either upper- or lowercase. *(Any set of letter flash cards will work.)* Hold a favorite classroom puppet in your hand. Let the child pick up letter cards and tell the puppet their names.

    A B C D E F G H I J K L M N O P Q R S T U V W X Y Z (or)
    a b c d e f g h i j k l m n o p q r s t u v w x y z

3. **Alphabet in random order:** Have the child read the scrambled letters in Box 2 on page 24 or 25.

    Z B F H Q O I G E J X D M A U L N R C K T S P W Y V (or)
    e y f p c x r b z a o d u j v l w i q k g m h s t n

Use the "Recording Responses" key (*see right*) as your guide on how to mark the checklists. This will allow you to see growth in how many responses a child gives as well as right and wrong responses.

> ## Recording Responses
> **O** each letter said correctly.
>
> **X** each incorrect response.
>
> **Underline** the letter when no response is given.

UPPERCASE LETTER IDENTIFICATION CHECKLIST

Child's name: _____

Teacher's name: _____

First assessment date: _____

Second assessment date: _____

Third assessment date: _____

1. **Letters in ABC order:** Have the child look at the complete alphabet in Box 1 and touch and read the letters.

A B C D E F G H I J K L M N O P Q R S T U V W X Y Z

2. **Small set of letters in random order:** Scatter a set of selected uppercase letter cards on a table surface. Hold a puppet in your hand. Let the child pick up letter cards and tell the puppet their names.

A B C D E F G H I J K L M N O P Q R S T U V W X Y Z

3. **Alphabet in random order:** Have the child read the scrambled letters in Box 2 at the bottom of the page.

Z B F H Q O I G E J X D M A U L N R C K T S P W Y V

A B C D E F G H I J K L M N
O P Q R S T U V W X Y Z

Box 1

Name the Letters

Z B F H Q O I

G E J X D M A

U L N R C K T

S P W Y V

Box 2

LOWERCASE LETTER IDENTIFICATION CHECKLIST

Child's name: _____

Teacher's name: _____

First assessment date: _____

Second assessment date: _____

Third assessment date: _____

1. **Letters in ABC order:** Have the child look at the complete alphabet in Box 1 and touch and read the letters.

   a b c d e f g h i j k l m n o p q r s t u v w x y z

2. **Small set of letters in random order:** Scatter a set of selected lowercase letter cards on a table surface. Hold a puppet in your hand. Let the child pick up letter cards and tell the puppet their names.

   a b c d e f g h i j k l m n o p q r s t u v w x y z

3. **Alphabet in random order:** Have the child read the scrambled letters in Box 2 at the bottom of the page.

   e y f p c x r b z a o d u j v l w i q k g m h s t n

 -

a b c d e f g h i j k l m n

o p q r s t u v w x y z

Box 1

Name the Letters

e y f p c x r

b z a o d u j

v l w i q k g

m h s t n

Box 2

ALPHABET KNOWLEDGE: AMERICAN SIGN LANGUAGE

The Effect of ASL on Increasing the Language and Literacy Skills of Young Hearing Children

Some of the most exciting research currently being conducted is focused on documenting the effects that learning sign language has on the development of language and literacy skills of young hearing children. It was observed that hearing children of deaf parents were often reading before they began school because their parents had fingerspelled with them. The researchers concluded that these children were able to make the connection between the manual letters of fingerspelling and the printed letters on a page. We have also learned a great deal about the importance of understanding and identifying the wide variety of individual learning styles as well as the importance of multisensory teaching. Sign language involves seeing, hearing, and movement. This is the perfect combination of how young children learn best. Using the multisensory approaches of sign language, children are able to use both sides of the brain, thus creating multiple pathways which can strengthen memory and build connections for further learning.

ASL Alphabet Letter Learning/Flash Cards—Pages 26–32

For each child, copy on card stock and cut out a set of ASL alphabet cards (pages 26–32). Each time a new alphabet letter in introduced, teach children the ASL sign for the letter. Also, teach the children how to fingerspell their names. As their literacy and fingerspelling skills increase, you can ask the children to figure out how to spell "secret" words. Begin by fingerspelling a CVC (consonant, vowel, consonant) word to a small group of students and have them record the corresponding letter symbols on paper. Then, repeat the steps, fingerspelling a second word that starts with a different consonant but ends with the same rime. When the letters have been recorded, tell the group your secret words and let them call out other rhyming words (actual or nonsense words).

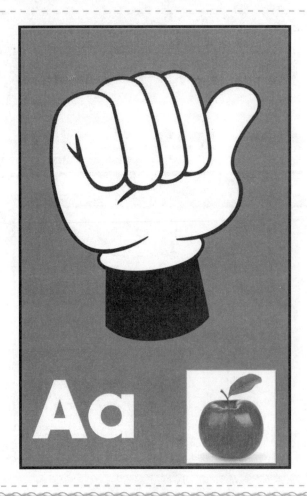

Cc

Dd

Ee

Ff

Gg

Hh

Ii

Jj

Kk

Ll

Mm

Nn

Oo

Pp

Qq

Rr

- 30 -

S s

T t

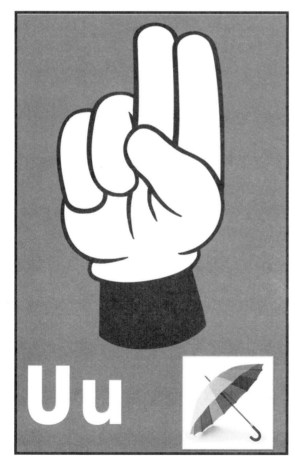

U u

V v

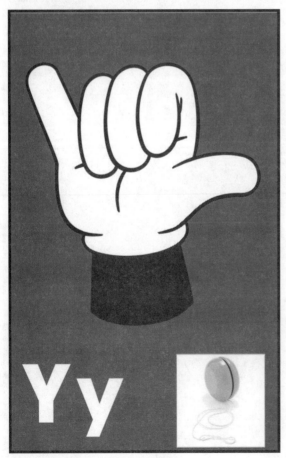

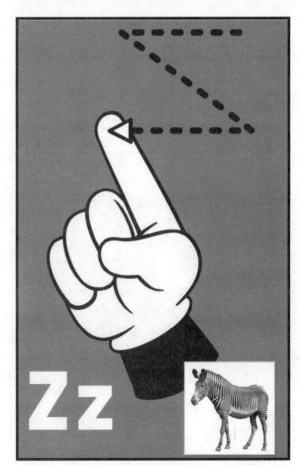

Ant and the Map

Directions: Cut along the dashed lines. Put the pages in order. Staple in the upper left-hand corner. Have children listen for the story's specific letter sound and then find and circle the featured letters.)

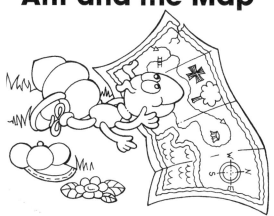

Little ant had a map.

-1-

Ant had to follow the path.

-2-

He ran and ran and ran.

-3-

Ant sat down. Can he last?

-4-

Ant had to go
back to the path.

-5-

Look! Many ants are
eating apples.

-6-

(Long Sound) Letter "Aa" Story

Ray and May Blue Jay

(Directions: Cut along the dashed lines. Put the pages in order. Staple in the upper left-hand corner. Have children listen for the story's specific letter sound and then find and circle the featured letters.)

Ray and May are blue jays.

They play all day.

They love to bake cakes.

They love to play games.

They love to paint on paper.

Ray and May make every day fun.

Letter "Bb" Story

Bobby Bear's Big Day

(**Directions:** Cut along the dashed lines. Put the pages in order. Staple in the upper left-hand corner. Have children listen for the story's specific letter sound and then find and circle the featured letters.)

Today is Bobby Bear's big day.

Bobby Bear got his bag.

Bobby Bear got his ball.

Bobby Bear got his bat.

Bobby Bear got his book.

Bobby Bear is playing baseball.

Letter "Cc" Story

Carly Cow Can

Carly Cow can cook.
Can you?

Carly Cow can cut.
Can you?

-3-

Carly Cow can count.
Can you?

Carly Cow can clean.
Can you?

-5-

Carly Cow can drive a car.
Can you?

Carly Cow can eat corn.
Can you?

KE-804080 © Key Education   - 36 -   *Early Literacy Intervention Activ*

Letter "Dd" Story

What Is Dog Doing?

(*Directions:* Cut along the dashed lines. Put the pages in order. Staple in the upper left-hand corner. Have children listen for the story's specific letter sound and then find and circle the featured letter.)

Did you see
the dog digging?

Yes, I did.
What is she doing?

Did you see
the dog digging?

Yes, I did.
What is she doing?

Did you see
the dog digging?

Yes, I did! Dog is digging
up a dinosaur bone!

(Short Sound) Letter "Ee" Story

Let's Help Hen

Directions: Cut along the dashed lines. Put the pages in order. Staple in the upper left-hand corner. Have children listen for the story's specific letter sound and then find and circle the featured letters.)

Let's help hen build a nest.

Elephant can help.

Elf can help.

Get a tent!

Hen cannot get wet!

Now, hen can rest in her nest

(Long Sound) Letter "Ee" Story

Can You See Me?

(**Directions:** Cut along the dashed lines. Put the pages in order. Staple in the upper left-hand corner. Have children listen for the story's specific letter sound and then find and circle the featured letters.)

Three bees play
hide and seek.

Can you see me?

The bees peek by the tree.

Can you see me?

The bees peek by the jeep.

See! Bee is sleeping.

Fox Is Fishing!

Fox is fishing.

(*Directions:* Cut along the dashed lines. Put the pages in order. Staple in the upper left-hand corner. Have children listen for the story's specific letter sound and then find and circle the featured letters.)

The fish fooled me!
It is a fan!

-3-

The fish fooled me!
It is a feather!

The fish fooled me!
It is a football.

-5-

I will get that fish!

Fooled again!
Fox fell in the water!

Letter "Gg" Story

Goat and Gorilla Giggle

(Directions: Cut along the dashed lines. Put the pages in order. Staple in the upper left-hand corner. Have children listen for the story's specific letter sound and then find and circle the featured letters.)

Goat and gorilla were good friends.

Everything they did made them giggle.

Good game, Goat!

They giggled playing games.

They giggled in the garden.

They giggled giving gifts.

They were giggly good friends.

Letter "Hh" Story

Hilda's Horrible Hat

-1-

(**Directions:** Cut along the dashed lines. Put the pages in order. Staple in the upper left-hand corner. Have children listen for the story's specific letter sound and then find and circle the featured letters.)

Hilda Horse said,
"How do I look?"

"It is a horrible hat,"
said Henry.

-3-

Hilda Horse said,
"How do I look?"

"It is a horrible hat,"
said Henry.

-5-

Hilda Horse said,
"How do I look?"

"Hooray! You have a hat I am
happy to eat," said Henry.

(Short Sound) Letter "Ii" Story

Little Baby Pig

This is little baby pig.

(**Directions:** Cut along the dashed lines. Put the pages in order. Staple in the upper left-hand corner. Have children listen for the story's specific letter sound and then find and circle the featured letters.)

Little baby pig is in his crib.

Little baby pig wears a bib.

Little baby pig wears a wig.

Little baby pig
dances a jig.

Silly little baby pig.

(Long Sound) Letter "Ii" Story

Five Mice

(**Directions:** Cut along the dashed lines. Put the pages in order. Staple in the upper left-hand corner. Have children listen for the story's specific letter sound and then find and circle the featured letters.)

Five mice like to ride bikes.

Five mice like to hike.

Five mice like to glide.

Five mice like to climb.

Five mice like to slide.

Five mice run
to the finish line.

Letter "Jj" Story

Who Can Jump?

(**Directions**: Cut along the dashed lines. Put the pages in order. Staple in the upper left-hand corner. Have children listen for the story's specific letter sound and then find and circle the featured letters.)

Can a jeep jump? No!

Can jam and jelly jump? No!

Can jacks jump? No!

Can a jet jump? No!

Can Joe and the
jack-in-the box jump? No!

Yes, they can!

Letter "Kk" Story

Katie Kitten and the King

(**Directions:** Cut along the dashed lines. Put the pages in order. Staple in the upper left-hand corner. Have children listen for the story's specific letter sound and then find and circle the featured letters.)

Katie Kitten
went to see the king.

Katie gave the king a kite.

Katie and the king
flew the kite.

The king was kind.

The king gave Katie
a key to the kingdom.

Katie kissed the king.

-1-

Look at the Little Friends

Look at little lion.

(*Directions:* Cut the pages along the dashed lines. Put the pages in order. Staple in the upper left-hand corner. Have children listen for the story's specific letter sound and then find and circle the featured letters.)

-2-

Look at little lamb.

-3-

Look at little lemur.

-4-

Look at the large box.

-5-

Let's build.

-6-

Look! A lemonade stand.

Mouse and Monkey

-1-

(Directions: Cut along the dashed lines. Put the pages in order. Staple in the upper left-hand corner. Have children listen for the story's specific letter sound and then find and circle the featured letters.)

Mouse and monkey want
to move to the moon.

-2-

They want to see
the man in the moon.

-3-

They made a map.

-4-

They put on moon masks.

-5-

They see
the man in the moon!

-6-

Where is
the man in the moon?
Did he move?

Letter "Nn" Story

(**Directions:** Cut along the dashed lines. Put the pages in order. Staple in the upper left-hand corner. Have children listen for the story's specific letter sound and then find and circle the featured letters.)

No, No, No! It Is Not Time!

"Is it time?" asked Ned.

"No, No, No.
Not yet." said Nellie.

"Is it time?" asked Ned.

"No! No! No!
Not yet!" said Nellie.

"Is it time?" asked Ned.

"Now, it is time," said Nellie.
Nine new babies!

(Short Sound) Letter "Oo" Story

A Lost Sock

(Directions: Cut along the dashed lines. Put the pages in order. Staple in the upper left-hand corner. Have children listen for the story's specific letter sound and then find and circle the featured letters.)

Fox lost her sock.

Is it in the pot?

Is it in the box?

Is it in the pond?

Is it by the log?

Stop, frog!
That is my sock!

(Long Sound) Letter "Oo" Story

Oh No! Joe's Bone!

Joe lost his bone.

(**Directions:** Cut along the dashed lines. Put the pages in order. Staple in the upper left-hand corner. Have children listen for the story's specific letter sound and then find and circle the featured letters.)

Use your nose!

The bone is not by the soap.

The bone is not by the boat.

The bone is not by the rose.

The bone is in the cone.

Porky Little Pigs

(Directions: Cut along the dashed lines. Put the pages in order. Staple in the upper left-hand corner. Have children listen for the story's specific letter sound and then find and circle the featured letters.)

-1-

Pass the peas, please.

-2-

Pass the pancakes, please.

-3-

Pass the potatoes, please.

-4-

Pass the pizza, please.

-5-

Pass the popcorn, please.

-6-

Pass the pillows, please.

Letter "Qq" Story

Quack, Quack!

Under the quilt!
Did you hear a quack?

(**Directions:** Cut along the dashed lines. Put the pages in order. Staple in the upper left-hand corner. Have children listen for the story's specific letter sound and then find and circle the featured letters.)

The queen
questioned the maid.

No, I think it was quiet.

Under the quilt!
Did you hear a quack?

The maid said,
"No, it is quiet!"

A quack from under the quilt.
Quiet, a baby duck!

Letter "Rr" Story

Rabbit
Runs
the Race

(**Directions:** Cut along the dashed lines. Put the pages in order. Staple in the upper left-hand corner. Have children listen for the story's specific letter sound and then find and circle the featured letters.)

Rabbit is
ready to run the race.

Ready, set, run!

Raccoon is ready
to run the race.

Ready, set, run!

Robin is ready
to run the race.

Round and round they run!

Letter "Ss" Story

Six Silly Seals

(*Directions:* Cut along the dashed lines. Put the pages in order. Staple in the upper left-hand corner. Have children listen for the story's specific letter sound and then find and circle the featured letters.)

Six silly seals
sat in the sun.

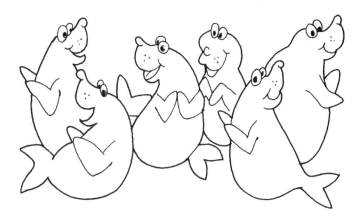

Six silly seals said,
"Let's have fun."

Some sailed on the sea.

Some played in the sand.

Some sat and sang.

Some played in the band.

Letter "Tt" Story

Two
Turtles

(*Directions:* Cut along the dashed lines. Put the pages in order. Staple in the upper left-hand corner. Have children listen for the story's specific letter sound and then find and circle the featured letters.)

Two turtles at play.

They have tons of toys.

They play with a top.

They play with a toy lion.

They watch TV.

Two tired turtles
are sleeping in a tent.

(Short Sound) Letter "Uu" Story

Suds in the Tub

(**Directions:** Cut along the dashed lines. Put the pages in order. Staple in the upper left-hand corner. Have children listen for the story's specific letter sound and then find and circle the featured letters.)

Cub played in the mud.

Duck played in the mud.

-3-

Bug played in the mud.

-4-

Fill the tub with suds!

-5-

Cub, duck, and bug
get in the tub.

-6-

Rub, rub, rub!

(Long Sound) Letter "Uu" Story

Cute Mule

(Directions: Cut along the dashed lines. Put the pages in order. Staple in the upper left-hand corner. Have children listen for the story's specific letter sound and then find and circle the featured letters.)

Cute mule works.

He uses a ruler.

He uses a tube of glue.

He uses a blue pencil.

What did cute mule make?

A flute to make music.

Letter "Vv" Story

A Very Special Day

-1-

(Directions: Cut along the dashed lines. Put the pages in order. Staple in the upper left-hand corner. Have children listen for the story's specific letter sound and then find and circle the featured letters.)

It is a very special day.

-2-

Vanessa Vulture vacuumed.

-3-

She put violets in a vase.

-4-

Vance Vulture
put on a vest.

-5-

He got his violin.

-6-

Happy Valentine's Day!

Letter "Ww" Story

Wendy and the Wagon

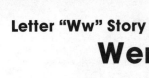

(**Directions:** Cut along the dashed lines. Put the pages in order. Staple in the upper left-hand corner. Have children listen for the story's specific letter sound and then find and circle the featured letters.)

Wendy has a new wagon.

She put a worm
in her wagon.

She put a walrus
in her wagon.

She put a watch
in her wagon.

She put a watermelon
in her wagon.

Wow! What a full wagon!

The Sound of "X"

(Directions: Cut along the dashed lines. Put the pages in order. Staple in the upper left-hand corner. Have children listen for the story's specific letter sound and then find and circle the featured letters.)

Not many words begin
with the letter "X."

There is "X-ray."

-3-

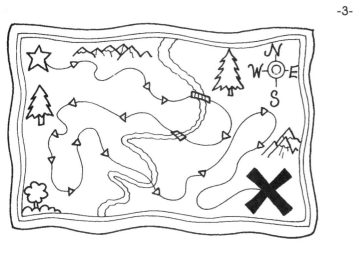

And, "X" marks the spot.

-4-

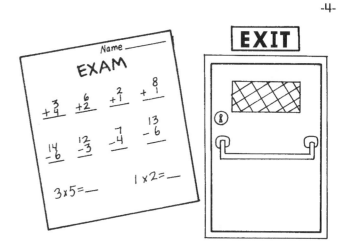

In "exam" and "exit,"
you can hear the "x."

-5-

"Box," "fox," "six," and "mix"
all have "x" at the end.

-6-

Can you hear the "x"
in "xylophone"?

Letter "Yy" Story

Yummy, Yummy!

Yanni Yak is hungry.

-I-

(Directions: Cut along the dashed lines. Put the pages in order. Staple in the upper left-hand corner. Have children listen for the story's specific letter sound and then find and circle the featured letters.)

-2-

He ate some yogurt.
Yummy, yummy!

-3-

He ate some yolks.
Yummy, yummy!

-4-

He ate some yams.
Yummy, yummy!

-5-

Yanni Yak is yawning!

Yummy, yummy!

Zoie's Zippy Toy

Zip, zap, zig, zag, zoom!

(**Directions:** Cut along the dashed lines. Put the pages in order. Staple in the upper left-hand corner. Have children listen for the story's specific letter sound and then find and circle the featured letters.)

-2-

Zoie, what is that
noise in your room?

-3-

Again,
zip, zap, zig, zag, zoom!

-4-

Zoie, what is that
noise in your room?

-5-

Again,
zip, zap, zig, zag, zoom!

-6-

I built a Zoie-bot
to clean my room.

KE-804080 © Key Education   - 63 -   *Early Literacy Intervention Activities*

Chapter 2
PHONOLOGICAL AWARENESS

The Alphabetic Principle

To further your knowledge of how children learn to read, it is necessary to understand that the English language is an **alphabetic system**—it uses written characters or symbols (graphemes) to represent sounds (phonemes) and sound patterns. However, it is not just a phonetic system. It is also an orthographic or spelling system that reflects meaning rather than just sounds. It is based primarily on the assumption that each speech sound or phoneme should have its own graphic representation. When a child develops an awareness of the relationship between sounds and letters and then begins to apply that knowledge to text, the child is understanding the concept of the alphabetic principle.

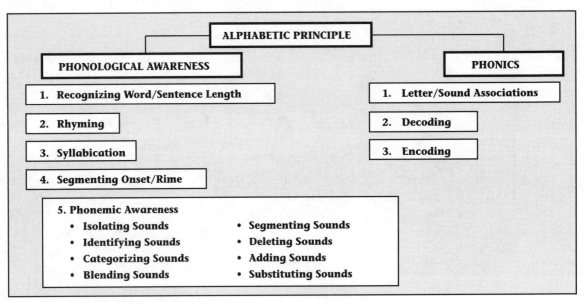

What Is Phonological Awareness?

Phonological awareness is the ability to understand that there are different ways that oral language can be divided into smaller components and manipulated. Spoken language can be broken down in many different ways, including:

- ◆ sentences can be broken down into words;
- ◆ words can be broken down into syllables (Divide the word *puppet* as /pup/ /pet/.);
- ◆ words can be broken down into onset and rime (Divide the word *cat* as /c/ /at/.);
- ◆ words can be broken down into individual phonemes (Divide the word *cat* as /c/ /a/ /t/.);
- ◆ words can be changed by manipulating sounds, such as adding, deleting, or substituting sounds. (Begin with the word *can*, add /l/ after the /c/ and the word is *clan*, delete the /c/ and the word is *an*, substitute /t/ for the /c/ and the word is *tan.*)

Students have phonological awareness when they have a basic understanding of all of these levels.

Why Is Phonological Awareness So Important?

Over the past 20 years, researchers have shown that phonological awareness in kindergarten is a strong predictor of later reading success. Many students with reading disabilities or students who are struggling readers have not acquired phonological skills and frequently have the most difficulty with phonemic awareness. The good news is that students who lack phonemic awareness can be identified and, with explicit instruction, they are able to improve their reading skills.

Phonological awareness is essential for reading success, and instruction in phonological awareness is beneficial for ALL children but can make or break reading success for struggling readers or at risk students. Phonological awareness instruction can begin as early as age four. These skills must be taught on a continuum and be age appropriate as well as fun, engaging, and motivational.

Instruction for Four-Year-Olds
- The student identifies letters and realizes that the letters represent parts of his own speech.
- The student understands that *fish* does not rhyme with *cow*.
- The student claps out syllables in familiar and unfamiliar words, such as *rob/in* or *el/e/phant*.
- The student can name several words that begin with the same sound, like *cat*, *cow*, and *can*.
- The student replaces one sound with another, for example, replacing the first sound in *fish* with /d/ to make *dish*.

By the End of Kindergarten
- The student can identify whether two single-syllable words rhyme.
- The student is able to think of two words that rhyme.
- When the student is reading a designated word and a list of three words, the student can identify which of the three words begins with the same sound as the designated word.
- When reading three words, the student can identify which word begins with a different sound than the other two words.

By the First Semester of First Grade
- The student can look at two-letter words (containing two phonemes) and blend the sounds together to read the word, for example, *at, in, on,* or *be*.
- The student can say the new word after a sound is dropped from the beginning or end of a three-phoneme word, for example, dropping the /r/ in *ran* and saying *an*.

By the End of First Grade
- The student can pronounce separately the sounds in two-phoneme words, such as /b/ /E/.
- The student can pronounce separately the first sound in longer words like the /c/ in *caterpillar*.
- The student can blend together the sounds in three-phoneme words like /d/-/i/-/g/ for *dig*.

Word Play Activities

Skill-building word-play activities are just as important as learning the names of the alphabet letters. Activities for strengthening receptive language skills are easy to plan and can be related to picture/photo cards, read-aloud books, nursery rhymes, favorite song lyrics, and so on. Plan sessions that target developmental needs of small groups of three or four preschoolers or slightly larger groups of kindergartners. Before you begin, write the children's names individually on large index cards and sort them into groups according to the oral language skill levels of the children. Keep a watchful eye on the time because the sessions do not need to be long—about six to eight minutes. Finally, at the end of each instructional session, be sure to record a few anecdotal notes on the cards regarding each child's progress.

What is the difference between phonological awareness activities and phonemic awareness activities? Phonemic awareness is only one aspect of phonological awareness and is concerned with the smallest unit of sound—the phoneme. Before planning your word-play sessions, quickly assess your students to find out if they can tell you how many words are in a spoken sentence, blend two words to make a compound word, identify rhyming words in a nursery rhyme, and count the syllables in words. All of these activities focus on larger units of speech sounds to strengthen phonological awareness.

PHONOLOGICAL AWARENESS: LISTENING SKILLS

The Importance of Developing Listening Skills

The ability to listen to environmental sounds is an important precursor to phonological awareness. Young students first need to be able to discriminate between sounds in the environment before they will be able to discriminate speech sounds.

> ### Listening skills include:
> - developing an awareness of sounds
> - being able to discriminate between different sounds
> - being able to remember what is heard
> - understanding what is heard
> - being able to sequence sounds
> - developing the ability to isolate one sound from another

Everyday Sounds

Help children recognize well-known sounds like the ones they hear at home. For this activity, you will need a tape or CD with different commonly heard sounds such as a tap running, a toilet flushing, a vacuum cleaner's motor, etc. Children will enjoy guessing what sounds they are hearing.

Outside Sounds—Page 67

Display a picture of a place such as a park, zoo, or airport. Then, ask children to think of the sounds they would hear if they were there. Make those sounds and record them. Play the tape on another day and let the children guess what they are hearing. (When using this activity in an ESL classroom, the next step would be to learn the proper vocabulary for the noises, such as *footsteps*, *honking*, etc.)

Variation: Use the two reproducible pictures provided on page 67 to help children further explore outside sounds. Copy a picture for each child. Ask children to circle everything in the picture that they think is making a sound. Then, discuss—and make—the sounds when they have completed their papers.

Now Hear This!

What you need: a variety of items that can be used to make noise, such as paper to crumple, a plastic glass and spoon to tap, a piece of chalk to write on a blackboard, two blocks to clap, a closed container filled with pebbles, a bottle to blow into, etc. Put each of the items in a small paper bag.

What you do: Choose one child to close or cover her eyes. Invite another child to select one of the bags, and, at a signal, make a noise with the contents. If the first child can guess what made the noise, she may have the next turn to choose a bag.

Variation: Place small musical instruments in the bags, such as a handbell, shaker, maraca, etc., or simply make noise-producing movements for the child to identify, such as clapping hands, snapping fingers, stamping feet, etc.

Matching Sounds

Fill small identical containers with rice, sand, small nails, salt, beans, cotton batting, etc., making two containers with each type of contents so that you have a pair of each. Have the children shake the containers and listen carefully to find each set of two that sounds the same.

Phonological Awareness—Listening Skills

At the Zoo

Name _____

✂ -

At the Playground

Name _____

PHONOLOGICAL AWARENESS: LISTENING SKILLS

Telephone

If possible, borrow two telephones or make do with toy phones and a teacher's creativity. Set up two "homes" or "offices" out of sight of each other (have children face away from each other or place one phone behind a screen). The children can introduce themselves over the phone and guess to whom they are talking. This activity will also provide a means of teaching proper phone etiquette.

Sounds through a Classroom Juice-Can Telephone

You will need two juice cans and a long piece of string. Make a hole in the bottom of each can. Thread one end of the string through each hole. Tie a knot or fasten the string around a toothpick inside of each can. Ask one child to hold one of the cans and give the other one to a partner. Have the children walk away from each other so that the string is pulled taut. One child may talk into his can while his partner puts her ear to the open end of the other can and listens. Ask, "How did the sound travel?"

Listen Carefully

Tell the children to close their eyes and be very quiet. Then, silently walk around the children, tap one on the shoulder, and whisper a request in that child's ear, such as to recite a nursery rhyme, sing a song, or simply say "hello, friends." That child then performs the request. When the child is finished, invite the other children to open their eyes and guess who was talking.

Listen to This!

Children are always fascinated with the voices they hear on a tape recorder, especially if the voices to which they are listening belong to them or to people they know. Make a tape of you telling stories or reciting finger plays. Provide a space where individual children can go off in a corner to replay their favorites. It is best if the recorder can be equipped with a headphone set. Then, let the children make tape recordings of themselves telling stories to listen to and enjoy.

Story Time Can Help Improve Listening and Attending Skills

Providing children with "before the story," "during the story," and "after the story" questions and conversation will help them become active listeners thereby improving their abilities to pay attention and concentrate.

Before the Story: Before reading a story to children, show them the book and discuss the cover. Point out the illustration on the front and talk about the author who wrote the book and the person who illustrated it. Tell students something engaging about the story to pique their interest. Providing children with some prior knowledge and getting them excited about the story will increase their listening and attending skills.

During the Story: As you read the story, ask questions and let children try to predict what will happen next. This ensures that children are listening in order to stay involved with the story. Continue to read and when you come to the answers for the questions you asked—or if the story just verified whether or not the children's predictions were correct—stop and review what the children had said or predicted about the story.

After the Story: When you have finished reading the story, discuss the ending with the children. Were their predictions accurate or was there a surprise ending? What clues were provided in the story that helped children come to their conclusions?

Play "Add-to-the-Story"

Choose one child to begin a story, for example, "Once upon a time there was a little frog who lived on a very little lily pad." Then, ask a second child to add another sentence to the story, such as, "The poor frog was just too big for the lily pad, so he decided to move." A third child may add another sentence, and so on. Each child must listen carefully in order to keep the story moving forward and make sense. This is a wonderful game to enhance listening skills. Choosing children to contribute in random order—and more than once—helps ensure that they will continue to listen closely throughout the activity.

Early Literacy Intervention Activities

PHONOLOGICAL AWARENESS: WORD AWARENESS

What Is Word Awareness?

The next important building block for learning how to read is to acquire word awareness. Children achieve word awareness when they understand that sentences consist of words and that these words can be manipulated.

According to Dr. Candace Goldsworthy, professor of speech-language pathology at California State University, Sacramento, word awareness is the first level of language analysis and must occur before children can begin the task of segmenting words into phonemes—the smallest sound components. When word awareness is first introduced to children, it is best to use content words (nouns) such as *bike*, *house*, *boy*, and *dog*. Children seem to more readily understand that these are individual words, rather than using words such as *the*, *and*, *at*, and *it*. Using content words in simple sentences will promote and strengthen children's understanding of the concept of word awareness.

Beginning Word Awareness Activities

Singing Exciting Songs

Sing songs that accentuate single words or have simple repetitive phrases, such as "Row, row, row your boat," "London bridge is falling down, falling down, falling down," or "Skip, skip, skip to my Lou."

Reading Stories Aloud

♦ **Point to the words.** Big books are wonderful to use when beginning to introduce word awareness. As you read aloud, point to each word. After the children have become familiar with the content of the story, let them take turns pointing to the words as you read them.

♦ **Fill in the missing words.** As you read a familiar story, stop and let the children fill in missing words. For example, when reading the book, *One Fish, Two Fish, Red Fish, Blue Fish* by Dr. Seuss, read the title as *One Fish, ____ Fish, Red Fish, ____ Fish*. Children should supply the words *Two* and *Blue*. Praise the children and tell them that they supplied the words that were needed.

♦ **What's the next word?** Pause on occasion when reading and pointing to the words in a big book and let the children "read" one of the words. Prompt the children by hesitating and then saying, "What word is next?"

Counting Words

First, practice counting with the children. Count how many children are in the class or how many windows are in the classroom. Next, explain that now you are going to count words.

Use familiar nursery rhymes or fairy tales so that children are already familiar with the content and the words used in the selection. For example, say, "How many words do you hear in this sentence? 'The sky is falling!'" The children would answer, "four." Or, use the wolf's phrase, "I'll huff and I'll puff." Children would then count five words.

Variation: To provide children with a more concrete experience, give each child five or six blocks. Have the children move a block forward for each word they hear. Then, have them repeat the sentence with you—touching a block for each word. Finally, count the blocks to "see" how many words were in the sentence. Alternatively, let children build towers with their blocks, placing one block for each word they hear. Repeat the sentence and challenge students to carefully remove one block at a time for each word.

PHONOLOGICAL AWARENESS: WORD AWARENESS

Story Dictation

Have children dictate their own sentences and then count the words as each sentence is read.

- ◆ **Dictate short high-interest stories.** Choose a story topic that you know will interest your students. Encourage them to generate sentences to create a story on the topic. Write the story sentences on chart paper or sentence strips. Be sure to write the words in exactly the same way the children say them. At first, keep the stories to four or five sentences, writing one sentence per line.

- ◆ **Learn about sentences.** This is the perfect time to introduce the concept of a sentence. Each time you write a sentence, clearly identify it as a sentence. It is also not too early to point out that the first word in the sentence begins with a "tall" or uppercase letter and that the sentence ends with a "dot" or period. Children will also notice that, as you write and read the words, you are moving from left to right.

Children Beginning to Recognize Words: Sentence Segmentation

This is a difficult task, but it is included in this section because sometimes children who have not yet begun to phonetically decode words may actually recognize whole words from activities like story dictation. Take the sentence strips children created during a story dictation (which should be sentences they know well) and cut each sentence into individual words (see below). Give one cut-up sentence to a group of children. Have children rearrange the words back into the original sentence and glue them onto another sentence strip. When the groups are finished, have each group read their sentence. Then, let the children decide which sentence came first in the story, which sentence was second, and so on until the original dictated story has been put back together in the correct order.

> There were three little pigs.

> pigs.   little   There   were   three

Counting Words in Books and Rhymes—Pages 33–63 and Pages 70 and 71

Use the reproducible Alphabet Mini-Books (pages 33–63) to give children more practice with word awareness. Copy, cut out and assemble the chosen mini-book for each child. Read a page to the children and have them pat their legs to count the words. Later, have them touch each word as you read it. You can also copy and hand out the reproducible rhymes (below and page 71) and use the same word counting techniques.

Counting Words Rhymes

Jack   be   nimble,
Jack   be   quick.
Jack   jump   over
the   candlestick.

**Red on top means,
stop, stop, stop.
Green below means
go, go, go!**

**Rain on the
green grass.
Rain on the tree.
Rain on the housetop
But not on me!**

**Hickory, dickory, dock,
The mouse ran up
the clock.
The clock struck one.
The mouse ran down,
Hickory, dickory, dock.**

PHONOLOGICAL AWARENESS: SYLLABLE AWARENESS

Recognizing Syllables

Now that children are aware of words as a whole, they need to realize that words are made up of units of sound called syllables. Being able to segment words into syllables helps the child learn about the structure of words.

Segmenting Syllables

Teaching syllable segmentation is important because children must learn that words are comprised of multiple sounds.

1. Clap and count the syllables in names. To introduce the children to syllables, lead them in counting the syllables in their own names. At first, model this activity by using several of the students' names, each with a different number of syllables, clapping each syllable as you say it. After each, ask the children how many syllables they heard. When they have begun to understand, invite the children one at a time to say and clap the syllables in their own names.

2. Feel the syllables. After the children can tell you how many syllables they have in their own names, have them hold two fingers under their chins. Ask them to speak their names. They will be able to feel their chins drop for each syllable spoken.

3. Stand up for syllables. Invite groups of children to take turns standing up according to how many syllables are in their names. First, let children in each group say their names aloud individually. Then, challenge each group to speak their names together in a chorus with each child saying his own name's syllables in unison with the others in the group.

Singing and Saying Compound Words with Two Beats

For a fun and easy way to introduce the concept of syllables, have children sing the following song and say simple compound words that have two beats. Children who are familiar with this song will quickly say the word to the beat of the music instead of clapping at the end of each line. Tell children what compound word to say or have them supply two-syllable words to use when singing the song. Examples include:

airplane	backyard	bedtime	birthday	corncob	football	mailbox	rooftop	snowball
anthill	bathtub	beehive	bookmark	doghouse	goldfish	notebook	sailboat	starfish
backdoor	beanbag	birdcage	bulldog	doorbell	haircut	popcorn	seagull	upstairs
backpack	bedroom	birdhouse	classroom	downhill	homework	rainbow	sidewalk	yardstick

If You Know a Compound Word, Say It Now!
(Sung to the tune of "If You're Happy and You Know It")
If you know a compound word, say it now. (cupcake)
If you know a compound word, say it now. (cupcake)
If you know a compound word, then your voice can say it loud.
If you know a compound word, say it now. (cupcake!)

PHONOLOGICAL AWARENESS: SYLLABLE AWARENESS

Syllable Shakers and Reproducible Picture Cards—Page 74

Have all of the children make their own syllable shakers. Use clean yogurt or margarine containers with lids and fill them partway with dried split green peas or rice to make noisemakers. Secure the lids with duct tape or shipping tape. Copy the syllable picture cards found on page 74. Print the numerals 1, 2, 3, and 4 individually on four pieces of card stock and lay the number cards on the table. Place the picture cards facedown in a pile in the center of the playing area.

Have children take turns drawing a card, saying the name of the picture on the card, and then repeating the name while shaking the container once for each syllable. Have the other players count the shakes and say their answers. Then, the child should place the picture next to the correct number card to show the number of syllables in the picture's name.

Variation: Read aloud a favorite picture book and select words from the text that have two or more syllables. Choose children to tell you how many beats (syllables) they hear when you say the words. To help them hear the syllables, encourage children to use their shakers when pronouncing the words.

Surprise Syllables

Fill a bag with lots of different small toys or classroom items. Let children take turns picking something out of the bag. The child should say the name of the object and then clap and count how many syllables are in the name of the object.

Syllable Sorting

Write the numerals 1, 2, 3, and 4 individually on each of four boxes and place them in front of the students. Explain that each number represents that number of syllables. Divide students into teams. Each team must search the room to find one object to place in each box. When all of the teams are finished, ask students to sit down. Then, go through the boxes together and decide if all of the objects in each box have the correct number of designated syllables.

Syllable Train

Reproduce the four train cards (below) for each student. Say a word with one to four syllables. Have the children put together their trains according to how many syllables they hear in the word.

Syllable Train Cars

Reproducible Syllable Picture Cards

(Directions are found on page 73.)

PHONOLOGICAL AWARENESS: RHYME AWARENESS

Rhyming Is One of the First Steps in Developing Phonological Awareness

Being aware of and recognizing rhyming words is a necessary step in learning to read. As young children become cognizant of the predictable language in books, such as *Brown Bear, Brown Bear, What Do You See?* by Bill Martin Jr. and illustrated by Eric Carle (Henry Holt and Company, 1992), they also begin to notice that certain words rhyme, for example, "Brown bear, brown bear, what do you *see*? I see a red bird looking at *me*." As you read aloud the remainder of the book, emphasize the rhyming words so that children's awareness of rhyme becomes sharper. In addition, as you foster this skill, select texts that feature common phonograms because the next step for emerging readers is to make the connection that some rhyming words end with the same letters.

Clapping and Snapping Games

Playing rhyming games and singing rhyming songs help children learn to pay attention to the sounds in words. Many songs and games include clapping, snapping fingers, bouncing, and tossing balls or beanbags. For example, combine rhythm and rhyming words with this pattern: clap, clap, snap (say, "cat"), clap, clap, snap (say, "hat"), clap, clap, snap (say, "rat"). Using real words is not important—what is important is that the spoken words rhyme with the other words.

Rhyming Word "Jump-Up"

Have children walk around the classroom. Say two words. When children hear a pair of words that rhyme, they jump up!

Let Loose—with Seuss and the Goose!

Mother Goose and Dr. Seuss probably never knew the positive impact their rhymes were going to have on teaching phonemic awareness. Besides simply enjoying their delightful rhymes, children can participate in specific activities that focus on rhyming patterns. (See Silly Rhymes and Rhyming Books on page 76.) The seven activities below can be completed with any nursery rhyme or any story that contains rhyming words.

- ◆ **Fill in the blank.** Read a familiar rhyme. Then, explain to children that you are going to read the rhyme again, but this time you will leave out some words. Pause at the end of a rhyming phrase and let children fill in the missing word, for example, "Jack and Jill, went up the _____."

- ◆ **Find new words.** Identify words that rhyme in the text (*Jill, hill*) and generate other rhyming words such as *pill, fill, dill,* and *Bill.*

- ◆ **Clap on the rhyme.** Clap every time a rhyming word is heard.

- ◆ **Record favorite rhymes.** Make a tape recording of the children's favorite rhymes.

- ◆ **Create illustrations.** Have children illustrate pairs of rhyming words such as *Jill* and *hill.* Point out the illustrations in the books that depict the words that rhyme.

- ◆ **Fill a rhyme box.** Fill a box in the classroom with rhyme books, puppets, and rhyme games.

- ◆ **Make up silly rhymes.** Review a traditional rhyme and then create a silly new rhyme with the same rhythm. For example, recite the rhyme, "Little Miss Muffet Sat on a Tuffet." Start again, changing the verse to "Little Brown Bear sat on a chair, eating a jar of honey. Along came a bee that flew onto his knee and said, 'Where is my money?' " It is also fun to make a recording of these original rhymes.

PHONOLOGICAL AWARENESS: RHYME AWARENESS

Silly Rhymes and Rhyming Books

Create silly rhymes with your students, the sillier the rhyme the better, such as "The flea didn't see the thorn in the tree and he sat on it—EEEEEEE!" This activity will help children listen for words that sound the same and identify rhyming patterns. Here are some stories to share that are written in rhyme:

Guarino, Deborah. *Is Your Mama a Llama?* Illustrated by Steven Kellogg. (Scholastic, 1989)

Hoberman, Mary Ann. *Miss Mary Mack.* Illustrated by Nadine Bernard Westcott. (Little Brown, 1998)

Hoberman, Mary Ann. *The Seven Silly Eaters.* Illustrated by Marla Frazee. (Harcourt, 1997)

Kirk, Daniel. *Skateboard Monsters.* Illustrated by the author. (Puffin, 1995)

Martin Jr., Bill. *Chicka Chicka Boom Boom.* Illustrated by Lois Ehlert. (Beach Lane Books, 2009)

Opie, Iona. *Here Comes Mother Goose.* Illustrated by Rosemary Wells (Candlewick Press, 1999)

Opie, Iona. *My Very First Mother Goose.* Illustrated by Rosemary Wells (Candlewick Press, 1996)

Seuss, Dr. *Green Eggs and Ham.* Illustrated by the author. (Random House, 1960)

Sierra, Judy. *Wild about Books.* Illustrated by Marc Brown. (Knopf, 2004)

Speed, Toby. *Brave Potatoes.* Illustrated by Barry Root. (Putnam, 2002)

Spinelli, Eileen. *The Best Time of Day.* Illustrated by Bryan Langdo. (Harcourt, 2005)

Yolen, Jane. *This Little Piggy and Other Rhymes to Sing and Play.* Illustrated by Will Hillenbrand. (Candlewick Press, 2005)

Name Games

Children love playing games that use their names.

- ◆ **Assign silly names.** Children think this game is very silly. Look at one child, for example, "Nate" and call him "Tate." Then, look at "Katie" and call her "Matie." Let children have fun thinking of new rhyming names for each other.
- ◆ **Sing "The Name Game."** It is also fun to teach children a song based on "The Name Game" by Shirley Elliston and Lincoln Chase (1964 EMI Al Gallico Music Corp.). Here is an example to get you going: Sherry, Sherry, Bo-Berry, Fee-Fi-Fo-Ferry, Sherry.

"Down by the Bay"

Listen to the traditional song "Down by the Bay," recorded by Raffi and available on *Singable Songs for the Very Young* (Rounder Records/UMGD, 1996), to help children become more aware of words that rhyme. Let children listen to and learn the words before introducing the concept of identifying the rhymes in each refrain. Give each child a musical instrument. Let them "make music" each time they hear a rhyming word.

Rhyming Pairs Memory Match—Page 77

Enlarge and copy, color, and cut out the rhyming picture cards on page 77. Lay the cards facedown on a table. Children should say the words aloud as they look and listen for the rhyming matches.

Take the Train

Choose one child to be the engineer. As the engineer begins to walk around the room, he stops beside another child and says a word. That child must say a word that rhymes with the engineer's word. Then, the two children walk together in a line, stop beside another child, and the engineer says a new word to rhyme. The game continues until everyone has joined the train. After a number of stops, choose a new engineer.

Rhyming Pairs Memory Match

(Directions are found on page 76.)

Pictures: *cat–bat, pig–wig, pen–ten, run–sun, king–ring, chair–hair, bee–tree, car–star*

PHONOLOGICAL AWARENESS: ALLITERATION—ISOLATING PHONEMES

What Is Alliteration?

Alliteration is the ability to recognize the initial sound of a word and relate this understanding to other words with the same initial sound. This ability relates to recognition of the sound rather than the letter.

Same Sounds—Alliteration

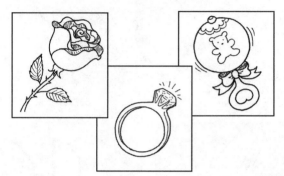

When children listening to a story have a breakthrough and start to recognize strings of words that begin with the same initial phoneme, you know that they are using their listening skills to detect finer differences in sounds. Many sentences in picture books and nursery rhymes feature names or groupings of two or more words that begin with the same sounds. This literary element is called *alliteration*.

It is very easy to include some experiences with alliteration in the curriculum by choosing rhymes for children to hear and recite anytime throughout the day. To make a listening activity fun during transition time, choose an alliterative name or phrase and change the wording of the rhyme if necessary. Then, direct children to stop and listen for your "magic word(s)" while you recite the rhyme. When they hear the magic word(s), they can then move to the new location.

- ◆ Little Tommy Tittlemouse lived in a little house; . . .

- ◆ Daffy-Down-Dilly has now come to town . . .

- ◆ Diddlety, diddlety, dumpty, the cat ran up the plum tree; . . .

- ◆ Peter Piper picked a peck of pickled peppers; . . .

- ◆ Lucy Locket lost her pocket, Kitty Fisher found it; . . .

- ◆ Wee Willie Winkie runs through the town, . . .

- ◆ Pease porridge hot, pease porridge cold, . . .

- ◆ Sing a song of sixpence, a pocketful of rye; . . .

- ◆ Fiddle-de-dee, fiddle-de-dee, the fly shall marry the bumblebee. . . .

- ◆ Diddle diddle dumpling, my son John went to bed with his trousers on; . . .

Alliteration to Sing

Share songs that play with sounds. *Singable Songs for the Very Young* and *More Singable Songs for the Very Young*, recorded by Raffi (Rounder Records/UMGD, 1996), are two CDs filled with delightful songs. One of the best examples is "Willoughby Wallaby Woo." The children can sing their own names and substitute the /w/ for the initial sound.

Willoughby Wallaby Wee, An elephant sat on me.	Willoughby Wallaby Watie, An elephant sat on Katie.	Willoughby Wallaby Weric, An elephant sat on Eric.
Willoughby Wallaby Woo, An elephant sat on you.	Willoughby Wallaby Wim, An elephant sat on Tim.	Willoughby Wallaby Warie, An elephant sat on Marie.

PHONOLOGICAL AWARENESS: ALLITERATION—ISOLATING PHONEMES

Tongue Twisters and Literature—Listening Carefully to Reading Aloud

While you are reading aloud, have children listen carefully for specific phonemes. To assist them, accentuate the phoneme you want them to identify. Use tongue twisters that feature the specific phoneme the children are learning. A list of tongue twister books can be found below.

Tongue Twisters and Alliteration

Choose a letter and then have children think of a sentence where almost every word begins with that same letter, for example, *T*—Todd told Ted to tip his top hat.

Here are several delightful tongue twisters:

Peter Piper picked a peck of pickled peppers.
Did Peter Piper pick a peck of pickled peppers?
If Peter Piper picked a peck of pickled peppers,
Where's the peck of pickled peppers
Peter Piper picked?

How much wood would a woodchuck chuck
If a woodchuck could chuck wood?
He would chuck, he would,
    as much as he could,
And chuck as much as a woodchuck would
If a woodchuck could chuck wood.

She sells seashells by the seashore.
The shells she sells are surely seashells.
So, if she sells shells by the seashore,
I'm sure she sells seashore shells.

A skunk sat on a stump and thunk
    the stump stunk,
but the stump thunk the skunk stunk.

Tongue Twister Books

The Animal Zone: Jokes, Riddles, Tongue Twisters & "Daffynitions" by Gary Chmielewski
    (Norwood House Press, 2007)

Elmo's Tricky Tongue Twisters by Sesame Street (Golden Books, 1999)

A Giant Little Book of Tongue Twisters by Joseph Rosenbloom and Mike Artell (Sterling, 2007)

Giggle Fit: Zany Tongue Twisters by Joseph Rosenbloom and Mike Artell (Sterling, 2005)

Oh Say Can You Say? by Dr. Seuss (Random House, 1979)

Super School Side-Splitters: A Tongue-Twister Tale by Quinlan B. Lee (HarperFestival, 2003)

Tongue Twisters to Teach Phonemic Awareness and Phonics: Beginning Consonants & Vowels by
    Joyce Kohfeldt (Carson-Dellosa, 2005)

Alliteration with Our Names

Use the students' names and create funny sentences about them, for example, Meagan makes many meatballs. Or, Paul paints and plays with play dough.

Make a Classroom Alliteration Counting Book

The students will enjoy making a classroom counting alliteration book. Here are some examples: 1 wild wolf, 2 tiny toads, 3 thankful thimbles, 4 frightened fairies, 5 fighting frogs, 6 sunbathing seals, 7 silly salamanders, 8 Asian ants, 9 naughty newts, and so on.

1 Wild Wolf

2 Tiny Toads

PHONOLOGICAL AWARENESS: ONSET—RIME

What Is Onset and Rime?

Onset is the initial consonant or consonant cluster of a word. **Rime** is the vowel and consonants that follow the onset. To introduce this concept, have the students place their two fists next to each other as they say a short word. (Use the Best Word Families and Rhyming Words for Beginners list at the bottom of the page for a word reference.) Then, have students move their fists apart to segment the onset from the rime.

Sliding to Blend Onsets and Rimes

Give children an onset, such as /g/, and the rime /-oat/. Have them put the two together and say "goat." Tell children to pretend that they are sitting at the top of a slide. They should say the onset at the top and hold that sound as they slide down. Once at the bottom, they say the rime. Use the Best Word Families and Rhyming Words for Beginners list at the bottom of the page for more words.

Slap, Slap, Clap!

Ask children to sit in a circle. Have them practice slapping their thighs twice (slap, slap,) and then clapping their hands together once. The rhythm would be **slap, slap, clap!** Then, use a variety of onset and rime words for the students to slap, slap, clap. Students should slap when saying the onset and rime and clap for the word when the two are combined, for example, /p/ (slap), /ig/ (slap), *pig* (clap); /d/ (slap), /og/ (slap), *dog* (clap); /r/ (slap), /at/ (slap), *rat* (clap); /h/ (slap), /en/ (slap), *hen* (clap); /p/ (slap), /et/ (slap), *pet* (clap).

——— Best Word Families and Rhyming Words for Beginners ———

-ag: bag, nag, rag, sag, tag, wag, brag, drag, flag	**-ell:** bell, cell, fell, Nell, sell, tell, well, yell, shell, smell, spell	**-ock:** dock, hock, knock, lock, rock, sock, block, clock, crock, flock, shock
-all: ball, call, fall, hall, mall, tall, wall, small, stall	**-en:** Ben, den, hen, Ken, men, pen, ten, then, when	**-ook:** book, cook, hook, look, nook, took, brook, shook
-ame: came, fame, game, lame, name, same, tame, blame, frame	**-et:** bet, get, jet, let, met, net, pet, set, wet, yet, fret	**-op:** bop, cop, hop, mop, pop, top, chop, drop, shop, stop
-an: ban, can, Dan, fan, man, pan, ran, tan, van, plan, than	**-ick:** Dick, kick, lick, Nick, pick, quick, Rick, sick, tick, wick, brick, stick, trick	**-ot:** cot, dot, got, hot, lot, not, pot, rot, tot, plot, spot
-and: and, band, hand, land, sand, brand, stand	**-ig:** big, dig, fig, jig, pig, rig, wig, twig	**-uck:** buck, duck, luck, muck, puck, tuck, Chuck, pluck, truck
-at: at, bat, cat, fat, hat, mat, rat, sat, chat, brat, that	**-ill:** bill, dill, fill, gill, hill, ill, Jill, kill, mill, pill, quill, sill, will, chill, drill, grill, spill, still	**-ug:** bug, dug, hug, jug, lug, mug, pug, rug, tug, plug, slug, snug
-eat: beat, eat, feat, heat, meat, neat, seat, cheat, treat	**-ine:** dine, fine, line, mine, nine, pine, vine, shine, spine, whine	**-ump:** bump, dump, hump, jump, lump, pump, rump, clump, grump, stump
-ed: bed, fed, led, Ned, red, Ted, wed, bled, fled, Fred, sled	**-ing:** bing, ding, king, ping, ring, sing, wing, bring, sting, swing, thing	
-eed: deed, feed, heed, need, reed, seed, weed, bleed, freed, speed	**-ip:** dip, hip, lip, nip, rip, sip, tip, zip, chip, drip, flip, ship, trip	

Early Literacy Intervention Activities

PHONOLOGICAL AWARENESS: PHONEMIC AWARENESS

What Is Phonemic Awareness and Why Is It So Important in Learning How to Read?

We have seen in the preceding pages that phonemic awareness is the ability to work with individual sounds, or phonemes, in spoken words. Phonemes are the smallest units of spoken—not written— language. Each child needs to understand that spoken words are made up of sounds and that new words can be created by combining, blending, and separating those sounds. The skill of phonemic awareness must be taught and developed before children can learn to read.

Phonemic awareness is the first true step in learning how to read and is the skill that children with reading disabilities have the most difficult time acquiring. Children who are unable to hear the phonemes in spoken words and cannot understand how a sequence of sounds forms individual words will, in all likelihood, have a difficult time equating specific sounds to the corresponding letters.

Phonemic awareness instruction benefits all children; however, effective instruction in phonemic awareness skills may actually make the difference between reading success and reading failure for over 20 percent of children.

The next logical instructional step after children demonstrate proficiency in **identifying rhyming words** and **recognizing syllables** is to help them **recognize individual sounds** in words (phoneme isolation) and **recognize the same sounds in different words** (phoneme identity).

It is advisable to follow these steps when teaching phonemes:

◆ First, teach the 16 consonants that have only one phoneme (*b, d, f, h, j, k, l, m, n, p, q, r, t, v, x, z*).

◆ Then, introduce those letters that have more than one sound (*c, g, s, w, y*).

◆ Next, add each vowel by introducing both of its sounds (long and short).

◆ Finally, add the digraphs that have two letters that create one sound (*th, wh, ch, sh*).

Beginning Phonemic Instruction

Some children enter kindergarten with an awareness of individual and the same sounds in words, even though they may not know which printed letters go with the sounds. Students may also segment by onset and rime and not by phoneme. Often, students need a lot of practice to be able to hear individual sounds.

By the end of kindergarten, students should be able to match same sounds, isolate the beginning and ending sounds in words, blend three sounds to make a word, segment the sounds in CVC words, and change a sound in a word to make a new word in songs and games.

Introducing Phonemes

Introduce phonemes with pictures, or visual clues; sound associations, or auditory clues, (for example, teach children the Campbell's soup commercial—"M'm! M'm! Good!®" for /m/, use a metronome or ticking clock for /t/, or make a buzzing sound, "zzzz" for /z/); and gestures and movements, or kinesthetic clues. The multisensory experience of visualizing pictures, using auditory clues (songs, rhymes, chants, etc.), and kinesthetic experiences can significantly help children learn to discriminate and isolate the phonemes— which will later help them make the connections between sounds and printed letters. (See pages 7 and 8 for ideas on visual, auditory, and kinesthetic methods for teaching letters.)

Looking in the Mirror

Let children watch themselves in a mirror as they say new sounds.

PHONOLOGICAL AWARENESS:
PHONEMIC AWARENESS—MATCHING & ISOLATING

After children have learned how to isolate initial and final phonemes in words, they will then be ready to identify other words that either begin or end with the same sounds. The following activities will focus on matching sounds word to word. A great resource of words that begin with the same letter is the collection of ABC books on your bookshelf.

Ideas to Introduce Phoneme Identification

Ask your students to sit in a circle. Have a set of real objects or picture cards whose names share the same phoneme in the beginning or ending position. Say the name of each object slowly, emphasizing the targeted sound. Ask two children to each choose an object or picture. Have both children say the names of their selected objects. Then, ask if the sounds at the beginning (or ending) are the same. Have students say the matching sound. Repeat until everyone has had a turn to choose an object.

I Spy Things for Sounds

For a fun and easy way to introduce the concept of matching initial phonemes, collect various common materials whose names begin with the same sound. Begin by locating two or three objects for each of these sounds: /d/, /f/, /l/, /m/, and /t/. Place the collected materials in the center of the playing area. Be sure to add a few objects to the collection that do not fit the criteria. Have children sit in a circle around the objects. Say, "I spy something that starts with the sound /m/." Children can point and take turns naming the objects (e.g, monkey, mouse, marbles, magnets). Continue the game as time and interest allow. Other groups of objects can be collected for these sounds: /h/, /k/, /n/, /p/, /s/, /b/, hard /g/, /v/, /y/, and /z/.

Let's Tell a Story!

Play the I Spy game again as directed above. At the end of each round, choose children to hold the named objects. Continue until everyone has been given an object. Then, invite the children to work in teams and make up an alliterative story (two or three sentences in length) about those objects. As children create their stories, remind them to include any other words they can think of that start with the assigned sound. Encourage them to look at ABC picture books for fun and even silly ideas. When the project is finished, have students tell their stories and act them out for the rest of the class.

Whose Name Begins with . . . ?

Here is another twist on the I Spy game. This time, ask questions that relate to the names of children in your classroom. If more than one child's name starts with the same sound, say, "I am thinking about someone whose name begins with (make the sound). Who is this person?"

Children may have to offer more than one answer before guessing the correct name. Alternatively, drop the initial phoneme and then say the name of the child. Invite the class to tell whose name you meant to say. For example, say, "I spy someone in the room whose name ends like _ayla. Who is this person?" (Kayla)

Sorting Board

Sorting Sounds—Pages 84–89

Reproduce the Sorting Sounds Cards found on pages 84–89 and the Sorting Board found on page 89. Children can sort the cards according to initial phonemes /b/, /d/, /f/, /g/, /h/, /j/, /k/, /l/, /m/, /n/, /p/, /r/, /s/, /t/, /v/, /w/, and /z/ and digraphs /ch/, /sh/, and /th/. Have children place the matching cards in one section of the Sorting Board.

PHONOLOGICAL AWARENESS:
PHONEMIC AWARENESS—MATCHING & ISOLATING

Odd One Out!

Select words that either begin or end with the same phoneme. Say the words to a small group of children. Have them simply listen carefully to the words the first time. Ask, "Which word has a different beginning (or ending) sound?" Repeat the words. When they hear the word that doesn't belong, have children make the signal for "out" by raising their hands and pointing with their thumbs just like a baseball umpire.

Where Is the Sound?

To help children visualize the placement of specific sounds in words, work with wooden blocks. Use the block labeled *B* or 1 to represent the beginning sound. Use the block labeled *M* or 2 to represent the middle sound, and use the *E* or 3 block for the ending sound. For example, ask a child, "Where is the /d/ in *dog*?" The child would then pick up the block labeled *B* or 1. Ask, "Where is the /g/ in *dog*?" The child would then pick up the block labeled *E* or 3.

"Ducks-in-a-Line" (First, Middle, and Final Sounds)

Enlarge and make a copy of the Ducks-in-a-Line patterns below for each child. Have children color their ducks and then cut them out. Help children arrange their ducks by explaining that ducks walk in a line. The mother duck is largest and first in line—she will stand for the first sound in a word. Then, the middle-sized duck will stand for the middle sound, and the little duck at the end of the line will stand for the final sound in a word. Ask various questions about the words while children answer the questions by pointing to the corresponding duck in their lines of ducks. For example, ask, "Where is the /d/ sound in *dog*?" Say the word again, sound by sound, /d/-/o/-/g/. Children should answer "The /d/ sound is at the beginning," while pointing to the mother duck. Ask about the position of other sounds in CVC words, such as, "Where is the /n/ sound in *ten*, /t/-/e/-/n/?" or "Where is the /a/ sound in *cat*, /c/-/a/-/t/?"

Alternatively, announce that the ducks in their lines are hungry, and it would be very fun to feed them. Give each child three paper cups, one for each of their ducks, and a small bowl of cereal and/or dried fruit. Each time you ask a question about a word, the child places a cereal piece in the cup of the corresponding duck. At the end of the activity, invite children to enjoy eating the snacks with their ducks.

Reproducible Sorting Sounds Cards

Pictures: Row 1: bed, bear, bike; Row 2: duck, deer, desk; Row 3: feather, football, fox; Row 4: goat, gum, gate

Reproducible Sorting Sounds Cards

Pictures: Row 5: hammer, hair, hose; Row 6: jacks, jump, jam; Row 7: kite, kangaroo, king; Row 8: ladder, leaf, lips

Reproducible Sorting Sounds Cards

Pictures: *Row 9: mice, marbles, mask; Row 10: nose, nest, nail; Row 11: pear, pie, puppet; Row 12: rose, rattle, ring*

Reproducible Sorting Sounds Cards

Phonemic Awareness—Matching & Isolating

Pictures: *Row 13: seal, sail, seeds; Row 14: tail, top, tape; Row 15: van, valentine, violin; Row 16: web, wagon, watch*

Reproducible Sorting Sounds Cards

Pictures: Row 17: zipper, zebra, zero; Row 18: chick, chest, cherries; Row 19: shark, sheep, shoes; Row 20: thread, think, thirty-three

17.

18.

19.

20.

Sorting Board

PHONOLOGICAL AWARENESS:
PHONEMIC AWARENESS—BLENDING PHONEMES

After children have learned to identify and isolate initial and final consonant sounds, challenge their thought processes by saying words in a segmented manner. For example, if you say /k/-/u/-/b/, have children repeat the sounds quickly until they can hear the word *cub*. Tailor the lessons by first determining how many phonemes the children will blend. For those children in kindergarten, select words that have either two or three phonemes. (See the two- and three-phoneme words in the Best Word Families and Rhyming Words for Beginners list on page 80.) Older students may handle words with up to four phonemes if blends and digraphs have been introduced. (See words to segment and blend on page 93.)

Blending Sounds with Busy Buzzy Bee—Page 92

Busy Buzzy Bee likes to help children learn how to blend sounds. Copy the picture of the bee on page 92 onto colorful card stock and cut it out. Make a Busy Buzzy Bee stick puppet by taping a craft stick to the back of the bee cutout.

Work with a small group of students. Select two or three pictures and arrange them on a flat surface in front of the children. For example, say, "Busy Buzzy Bee wants one of these pictures. Listen carefully to what I say: /c/-/a/-/p/. Which picture does Busy Buzzy Bee want?" Children should then choose the picture of a cap. Repeat the activity with other picture cards.

Blending Blocks

This activity helps students learn how to see, feel, and hear the sounds in a word. Demonstrate the following steps before children try to blend the sounds. First, show children two blocks of different colors. Explain that each block represents a sound. Touch one block as you say /m/. Then, touch another block and say /E/. (Remember to always demonstrate from left to right as if you are "reading" the sounds.) Finally, touch and move the first block, stretching out the sound /mmmm/ as you slide it toward the second block. Then, when the first block touches the second block, say /EEEE/. The children can hear, feel, and see that the word is *me*. Begin with words containing two phonemes and work up to words with three or more individual sounds.

Say It Slowly, Say It Fast!—Page 92

This fun activity can help children learn how to blend phonemes. Copy the turtle and the rabbit puppet patterns found on page 92. The children can color, cut out, and create puppets by taping them onto craft sticks.

Fill a box or bag with small toys or classroom objects. Pick an object out of the bag, hold up a turtle puppet, and say the object's name just like the turtle would—very slowly. Then, have the children repeat the word back to you just like the rabbit would—very fast while holding up their rabbit puppets. Repeat in reverse by saying the word quickly and having the children respond slowly.

Finally, when children thoroughly understand the unique workings of phonemes, they will understand that the sequencing and then blending of spoken phonemes create words.

Surprise Bag

Fill a bag with classroom objects. Pick an object out of the bag and say its name slowly so that each phoneme is heard. Choose a child to repeat the name, blending the sounds to make the word. That child is next to pick an object from the bag. Again, say the object's name, emphasizing individual sounds. The child chooses a friend to blend the phonemes. Continue until all of the objects have been named.

PHONOLOGICAL AWARENESS:
PHONEMIC AWARENESS—BLENDING PHONEMES

Real Sliding

Take learning outside to your school's playground. Provide children with two- or three-phoneme words before they go down the slide. At the top of the slide, the child should say each phoneme in the word separately. When the child reaches the bottom of the slide, he quickly blends the phonemes to say the whole word.

Objects in the Room

Say the sounds for the name of an object in the classroom, such as /c/-/l/-/o/-/k/. Stretch the sounds so that students must do the auditory processing to blend the sounds together. Then, ask students to identify the object—*clock.*

As students become more comfortable with blending sounds, let them move plastic alphabet letters as they hear the sounds. Start by sounding out simple CVC words or CCVC words to help them begin to connect sounds with graphemes. Slowly say the sounds of a word. Students should move the letters that correspond to the sounds.

Help the Robot Talk

Copy the robot puppet pattern below. Color, cut out, and tape the robot to the front of a small, clean milk carton. Create a pile of small pictures representing words with two and three phonemes. Let children take turns choosing a picture from the pile. Say the name of the object slowly, for example, "You chose a /h/-/a/-/t/." The child should repeat the sentence in a robot voice, blending the phonemes together, "I chose a *hat.*"

Robot Puppet Pattern

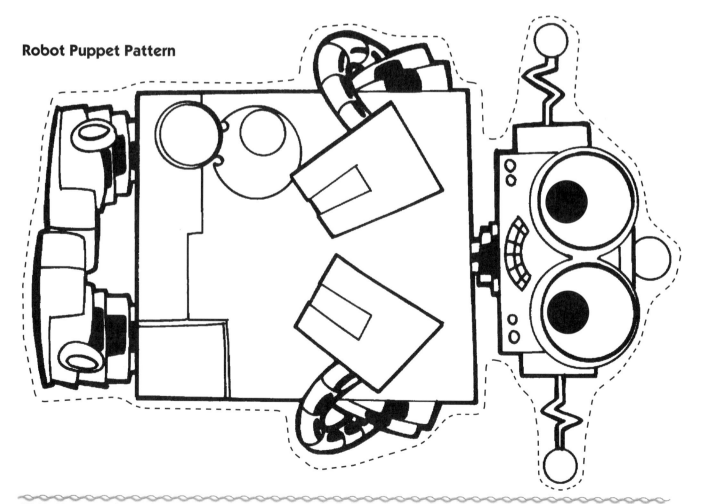

 Early Literacy Intervention Activities

PHONOLOGICAL AWARENESS: PHONEMIC AWARENESS—SEGMENTING PHONEMES

When children can demonstrate the skill of blending isolated phonemes to create words, have them do the reverse skill: listening to whole words and then separating the sounds in those words. **Phoneme segmentation** is asking the student to separate a word into its speech sounds, or phonemes. For example, remind students that every word is made up of sounds. Then, say, "Listen to this word: *dog*—/d/-/o/-/g/. Let's count the sounds in the word *dog*—/d/-/o/-/g/." Have students use their fingers or move a block for each sound they hear in the word.

Segmenting and Blending Picture Puzzle Cards—Page 95

This is a wonderful activity for children to visually see how words can be blended together and then segmented or taken apart. Copy, color, cut out, and laminate the Picture Puzzle Cards provided on page 95 or use any picture cards of your choice for this activity.

Cut each picture card into the same number of pieces as its phoneme sounds. Place the pieces for each card in a pile. A student chooses a card pile and then put the picture together, leaving spaces between the parts (as illustrated). The student names the picture (*shark*). Then, while sliding the parts together, she should say the phonemes (/sh/-/a(r)/-/k/). When the picture is together, she should say the word again (*shark*). This fun, self-checking activity allows children to visualize the word being blended, taken apart into its phonemes, and then put back together again.

I Spy Segmenting and Blending

Play a variation of I Spy to develop your students' skills in segmenting and blending phonemes. Begin by saying to the class, "I spy something in our room. Listen carefully to its name because I'm going to say its name a silly way. I spy a /f/-/i/-/sh/. Can you guess what it is?"

After children have practiced blending sounds, vary the I Spy game by inviting children to choose and segment words for you to blend. Begin by using words with only two or three individual sounds and work up to words with four or more sounds, such as /b/-/r/-/i/-/k/ (*brick*).

Following are examples of words for students to segment and blend.

ape	book	broom	desk	fish	moose	phone	soap	truck
ball	bow	cap	dog	glass	pan	shoe	stool	wig
barn	bread	cat	dress	ice	pea	skate	tie	web
bean	brick	cheese	eel	jump	pen	slip	train	zoo

Working in Pairs—Page 96

Have students work with partners. Each partner team will need a set of game cards found on page 96. As a whole class, say the name of each picture, segment the word into its individual phonemes, and finally count how many phonemes are in the word. Have one of the partners write the correct number of phonemes on the back of each of the game cards.

Now, the children can work as teams. They should pick up a card, say the word together, segment the word into phonemes, count the phonemes, and then self-check their answers by looking on the back of the card. Have the partners place all of the cards they segmented correctly in one pile and cards that need additional practice in another pile. Children love to be able to check their own responses. It also helps build self-confidence when they can see how often their answers were correct. You will also find it valuable to check your students' card piles to see which words need additional practice. You may see a pattern in the phonemes that students are not hearing or processing accurately.

PHONOLOGICAL AWARENESS:
PHONEMIC AWARENESS—BLENDING PHONEMES

Phoneme Count Hopscotch

Create a traditional hopscotch pattern, either with chalk outdoors or with masking tape in your classroom. Say a word and then have a child count out the phonemes as he hops on the hopscotch squares. For example, if the word is *cow*, the student would say /k/ and hop on the number 1 and then say /ow/ and hop on the number 2. The last number reinforces the total number of phonemes heard in the word.

Phoneme Beanbag Toss

Draw a four-square grid with chalk outside or use masking tape inside. Write 1, 2, 3, or 4 in each square. Have a pile of picture cards representing words with one to four phonemes ready for the children. The first child tosses the beanbag onto one of the numerals. For example, if the child's beanbag lands on 3, the child should look through the pictures and find one whose name has three phonemes. This activity is much more difficult than simply being asked to segment a particular word. The children must analyze several cards before choosing one that matches the same number of phonemes as the number on which the beanbag landed.

Phonemes in Our Names

Collect a photograph of each child, tape the photos on sheets of paper, and then photocopy them to create picture cards. Follow the directions for the Working in Pairs activity on page 93, but make game cards using the children's photos and names. This variation may require a higher level of skill as students count the phonemes in the multisyllable names of their classmates.

Banking on Sounds

Each student will need a copy of the Banking on Sounds Piggy Bank Pattern (below) and at least 10 pennies. Generate words from classroom materials or from a favorite children's book. As you say a word, children should place a penny "in" the piggy bank for each phoneme they hear.

**Banking on Sounds
Piggy Bank Pattern**

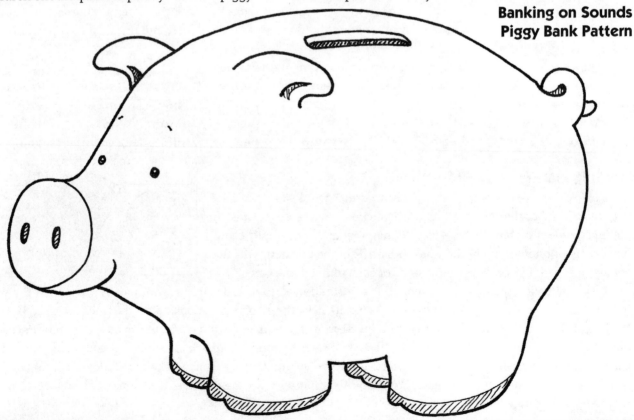

Reproducible Picture Puzzle Cards

card 1

card 5

card 2

card 6

card 3

card 7

card 4

card 8

Answer key: 1. /k/ /ow/   2. /b/ /E/   3. /b/ /O/ /t/   4. /sh/ /a(r)/ /k/   5. /f/ /i/ /sh/   6. /b/ /l/ /o/ /k/   7. /f/ /r/ /o/ /g/   8. /t/ /i/ /g/ /u(r)/

Reproducible Working in Pairs Game Cards

Phonemic Awareness—Segmenting Phonemes

Pictures: *Row 1: dog, fish, fan, car; Row 2: jar, box, book, drum;*
Row 3: rope, cheese, chair, peach; Row 4: pig, coat, key, kite; Row 5: cow, star, jet, slide

Early Literacy Intervention Activities

PHONOLOGICAL AWARENESS:
PHONEMIC AWARENESS—MANIPULATING PHONEMES

The most difficult skills when changing individual sounds in spoken words are to substitute, delete, and add phonemes to build new words. Only after children have had rich experiences working with rhyming words, recognizing alliterative phrases, isolating sounds, and blending and segmenting phonemes would it be appropriate for them to manipulate phonemes in word-play games and lessons. The following examples explain further how to use these advanced phonemic awareness skills:

◆ **Phoneme substitution is when one phoneme is substituted for another phoneme. For example, begin with the word *bug*. Change /b/ to /m/, and the word *bug* is changed to *mug* or change /g/ to /n/, and the word *bug* is changed to *bun*.**
To practice this skill, first have children answer word riddles using initial consonants as onsets with rimes. Then, proceed to riddles that incorporate initial blends and digraphs as onsets. (See the Best Word Families and Rhyming Words for Beginners list on page 80 for onset and rime ideas.) For example, ask: What word begins with /m/ and rhymes with *top*? (*mop*) What word begins with /dr/ and rhymes with *top*? (*drop*) What word begins with /ch/ and rhymes with *top*? (*chop*)

◆ **Phoneme deletion is when one phoneme is removed, leaving a different, recognizable word. For example, the word *block* without /b/ is *lock*, or the word *cart* without /t/ is *car*.**
When children can easily hear and count individual phonemes in words, then they are ready to try deleting sounds to make new words. For example: Take away the /f/ sound in the word *flock*. What is the new word? (*lock*) Take away the /t/ sound in the word *train*. What is the new word? (*rain*) The answers do not always have to be actual words. For additional practice, have children answer riddles like these: What "word" would be left if you take away the /k/ sound in *snack*? (*sna*) If you take away the /s/ sound in *snack*? (*nack*) For another example, ask: What word do you have if you take away the /p/ sound in *clamp*? (*clam*) If you take away the /k/ sound in *clamp*? (*lamp*) If you take away the /l/ sound in *clamp*? (*camp*)

◆ **Phoneme addition is when a new word is made by adding a phoneme to the original word. For example, add /s/ to the beginning of *tar* to change the word to *star* or add /t/ to the end of *tar* to change the word to *tart*.**
To strengthen this skill, generate riddles that ask children to add certain sounds to chosen phonograms or words. This type of exercise is also an effective way to introduce a read-aloud book that incorporates wonderful language play in its title. Check your bookshelf for potential activity ideas. For example, before reading aloud the book *Smash! Mash! Crash! There Goes the Trash!* by Barbara Odanaka, think of word riddles for the -ash family. Examples include the following: What word rhymes with *ash* and begins with /b/? (*bash*) Begins with /d/? (*dash*) Begins with /l/? (*lash*) What word do you have if you add /f/ to *lash*? (*flash*) If you add /s/? (*slash*) If you add /k/? (*clash*) What word do you have if you add /s/ to *mash*? (*smash*) If you add /t/ to *rash*? (*trash*) If you add /k/? (*crash*) After this fun word play activity, everyone will be ready to read more about trash!

Play Add-On and Take Away

Give children words and ask them to repeat the word minus a sound or with an additional sound. For example, take away the /k/ from *monkey* to make what word? (*money*) Add /l/ to *feet* to make what word? (*fleet*)

PHONOLOGICAL AWARENESS: PHONEMIC AWARENESS—MANIPULATING PHONEMES

Sample Read-Aloud Books

No doubt, there are wonderful picture books with delightful language play already on your bookshelf. Try to locate titles with lively story lines, rhyming patterns, or strings of nonsense words that draw attention to sounds. Here are some excellent selections which are perfect for practicing the manipulation of phonemes.

- *The Cow That Went Oink* by Bernard Most (Harcourt Brace Jovanovich, 1990)
- *Rub-a-Dub Sub* by Linda Ashman (Harcourt Brace Jovanovich, 2003)
- *Rattletrap Car* by Phyllis Root (Candlewick Press, 2001)
- Dr. Seuss titles—choose your favorites!

Sing Songs

Sing familiar songs and change the phonemes in the chorus. For example, change the *ee-i-ee-i-o* in "Old MacDonald" to *mee-i-mee-i-toe* or change the chorus in "The Farmer in the Dell" from *hi-ho-the-dario, the farmer in the dell* to *di-do-the-mario, the charmer in the well*. Children will giggle as they think of funny new choruses for the songs they know. Continue to help children gain experience with recognizing that when a phoneme is removed, added, or substituted, a new word is created. Use the examples below to get started.

Phoneme Manipulation Examples

Here are some words to use when practicing with students:

Deletion of Beginning Phonemes
the word: *blast*—take away /b/ = *last*
the word: *bread*—take away /b/ = *read*
the word: *candy*—take away /k/ = *Andy*
the word: *cow*—take away /c/ = *ow*
the word: *deer*—take away /d/ = *ear*
the word: *farm*—take away /f/ = *arm*
the word: *feet*—take away /f/ = *eat*
the word: *gate*—take away /g/ = *ate*
the word: *leg*—take away /l/ = *egg*
the word: *seal*—take away /s/ = *eel*
the word: *skid*—take away /s/ = *kid*
the word: *smile*—take away /s/ = *mile*
the word: *tape*—take away /t/ = *ape*
the word: *tie*—take away /t/ = *I or eye*
the word: *towel*—take away /t/ = *owl*

Deletion of Final Phonemes
the word: *bean*—take away /n/ = *bee*
the word: *boat*—take away /t/ = *bow*
the word: *boil*—take away /l/ = *boy*
the word: *bowl*—take away /l/ = *bow*
the word: *cart*—take away /t/ = *car*
the word: *dollar*—take away /a(r)/ = *doll*
the word: *ice*—take away /s/ = *I or eye*
the word: *pillow*—take away /O/ = *pill*
the word: *pipe*—take away /p/ = *pie*
the word: *shelf*—take away /f/ = *shell*
the word: *team*—take away /m/ = *tea*

Addition of Beginning Phonemes
the word: *ear*—add /t/ = *tear*
the word: *ice*—add /r/ = *rice*
the word: *it*—add /s/ = *sit*
the word: *lake*—add /f/ = *flake*
the word: *lap*—add /c/ = *clap*
the word: *last*—add /b/ = *blast*
the word: *lid*—add /s/ = *slid*
the word: *lock*—add /c/ = *clock*
the word: *nail*—add /s/ = *snail*
the word: *pace*—add /s/ = *space*
the word: *rain*—add /t/ = *train*
the word: *top*—add /s/ = *stop*

Substitution of Beginning Phonemes
the word: *bike*—change /b/ to /l/ = *like*
the word: *bone*—change /b/ to /f/ = *phone*
the word: *cake*—change /k/ to /r/ = *rake*
the word: *cat*—change /k/ to /r/ = *rat*
the word: *cot*—change /k/ to /d/ = *dot*
the word: *dice*—change /d/ to /m/ = *mice*
the word: *dog*—change /d/ to /f/ = *fog*
the word: *fan*—change /f/ to /k/ = *can*
the word: *goat*—change /g/ to /b/ = *boat*
the word: *hen*—change /h/ to /p/ = *pen*
the word: *hose*—change /h/ to /r/ = *rose*
the word: *house*—change /h/ to /m/ = *mouse*
the word: *ring*—change /r/ to /w/ = *wing*
the word: *ten*—change /t/ to /h/ = *hen*

Substitution of Final Phonemes
the word: *bun*—change /n/ to /t/ = *but*
the word: *bus*—change /s/ to /g/ = *bug*
the word: *can*—change /n/ to /t/ = *cat*
the word: *cow*—change /ow/ to /E/ = *key*
the word: *doll*—change /l/ to /k/ = *dock*
the word: *fat*—change /t/ to /n/ = *fan*
the word: *fin*—change /n/ to /sh/ = *fish*
the word: *five*—change /v/ to /l/ = *file*
the word: *game*—change /m/ to /t/ = *gate*
the word: *kiss*—change /s/ to /ng/ = *king*
the word: *pig*—change /g/ to /n/ = *pin*
the word: *rail*—change /l/ to /n/ = *rain*
the word: *sent*—change /t/ to /d/ = *send*
the word: *wish*—change /sh/ to /ng/ = *wing*

Substitution of Medial Phonemes
the word: *bat*—change /a/ to /e/ = *bet*
the word: *bell*—change /e/ to /i/ = *bill*
the word: *bike*—change /I/ to /A/ = *bake*
the word: *boot*—change /OO/ to /a/ = *bat*
the word: *cat*—change /a/ to /i/ = *kit*
the word: *cub*—change /u/ to /a/ = *cab*
the word: *mile*—change /I/ to /U/ = *mule*
the word: *moon*—change /OO/ to /a/ = *man*
the word: *pail*—change /A/ to /OO/ = *pool*
the word: *phone*—change /O/ to /i/ = *fin*
the word: *pin*—change /i/ to /e/ = *pen*

Substituting Phonemes: Three Different Activities

Name:

Substituting Beginning Phonemes
1. *cat* change /c/ to /b/ = *bat*
2. *dog* change /d/ to /l/ = *log*
3. *pail* change /p/ to /n/ = *nail*
4. *cub* change /c/ to /t/ = *tub*
5. *pen* change /p/ to /h/ = *hen*
6. *bug* change /b/ to /r/ = *rug*
7. *pig* change /p/ to /w/ = *wig*
8. *boat* change /b/ to /g/ = *goat*

Substituting Final Phonemes
1. *cat* change /t/ to /n/= *can*
2. *dog* change /g/ to /l/ = *doll*
3. *pail* change /l/ to /n/ = *pain*
4. *cub* change /b/ to /t/ = *cut*
5. *pen* change /n/ to/t/ = *pet*
6. *bug* change /g/ to /s/ = *bus*
7. *pig* change /g/ to /n/ = *pin*
8. *boat* change /t/ to /n/ = *bone*

Substituting Medial Phonemes
1. *cat* change /a/ to /u/ = *cut*
2. *dog* change /o/ to /i/ = *dig*
3. *pail* change /A/ to /OO/ = *pool*
4. *cub* change /u/ to /a/ = *cab*
5. *pen* change /e/ to /a/ = *pan*
6. *bug* change /u/ to /a/ = *bag*
7. *pig* change /i/ to /e/ = *peg*
8. *boat* change /O/ to /a/ = *bat*

Assessment: Phonemic Awareness

Student's Name: _____

Assessed by: _____

1st Assessment Date: _____

2nd Assessment Date: _____

3rd Assessment Date: _____

The Phonemic Awareness Assessment is designed to be used as an informal assessment tool to assist teachers in determining each student's understanding of phonemic awareness, including specific skills that have been mastered and skills that are not as yet understood. The following assessment can be used as a pre-test, posttest, and to provide documentation of the progress of each stuident.

This is an oral assessment. Reproduce pages 100 and 101 for each student and record the student's reponses as you administer the assessment. If you see that the child is struggling and misses more than 3 questions in a section, skip the remaining part of that section and move to the next. Mark each box according to the student's response.

1. Rhyming Words

Listen carefully. I am going to say two words: *cat* and *mat*. These words rhyme because they have the same ending sound. The words *cat* and *mouse* do not rhyme. *(Model more examples if the student looks unsure.)* I am going to say some more words. You can say "yes" if you think the words rhyme or "no" if you do not think the words rhyme.

a. dog – hog ☐ correct ☐ incorrect   e. mice – nice ☐ correct ☐ incorrect

b. sun – fun ☐ correct ☐ incorrect   f. cow – can ☐ correct ☐ incorrect

c. dog – frog ☐ correct ☐ incorrect   g. pan – ran ☐ correct ☐ incorrect

d. map – cot ☐ correct ☐ incorrect   h. look – book ☐ correct ☐ incorrect

Subtotal ☐ correct ☐ incorrect

2. Recognizing Syllables

Listen carefully. I am going to say a word, clap my hands, and count each syllable—demonstrate cupcake, with two caps, and then say "two." *(Model more examples if the student looks unsure.)* Are you ready? I will say a word and then you repeat the word, clap, and count how many syllables are in the word.

a. fish ☐ correct ☐ incorrect   e. but – ter – fly ☐ correct ☐ incorrect

b. desk ☐ correct ☐ incorrect   f. mon – key ☐ correct ☐ incorrect

c. ta – ble ☐ correct ☐ incorrect   g. di – no – saur ☐ correct ☐ incorrect

d. ro – bin ☐ correct ☐ incorrect   h. pup – py ☐ correct ☐ incorrect

Subtotal ☐ correct ☐ incorrect

3. Matching Beginning Phonemes

Listen carefully. I am going to say three words: *boy, baby,* and *bat*. These words all begin with the same sound /b/. *(Model more examples if the student looks unsure.)* Now, I will say three more words— two of the words have the same beginning sound. You are to tell me which two words begin with the same sound.

a. bike – face – bear ☐ correct ☐ incorrect   d. jacks – leaf – jump ☐ correct ☐ incorrect

b. duck – deer – goat ☐ correct ☐ incorrect   e. top – moon – me ☐ correct ☐ incorrect

c. gum – fan – foot ☐ correct ☐ incorrect   f. pear – pie – house ☐ correct ☐ incorrect

Subtotal ☐ correct ☐ incorrect

4. Isolating Beginning Phonemes

Listen carefully. I am going to say a word. I would like you to tell me the first sound of the word. If I said, *"top,"* you would say /t/. *(Model more examples if the student looks unsure.)* Repeat each word and then say the first sound.

a. kite /k/ ☐ correct ☐ incorrect   e. man /m/ ☐ correct ☐ incorrect

b. bike /b/ ☐ correct ☐ incorrect   f. doll /d/ ☐ correct ☐ incorrect

c. house /h/ ☐ correct ☐ incorrect   g. seal /s/ ☐ correct ☐ incorrect

d. rose /r/ ☐ correct ☐ incorrect   h. lamp /l/ ☐ correct ☐ incorrect

Subtotal ☐ correct ☐ incorrect

~~~~~~

5. Matching Final Phonemes

Listen carefully. I am going to say three words: *tent, bat,* and *foot.* These words all have the same ending sound /t/. *(Model more examples if the student looks unsure.)* Now, I will say three more words— two of the words have the same ending sound. You are to tell me which two words end with the same sound.

a. web – tub – can ☐ correct ☐ incorrect   d. mop – hen – can ☐ correct ☐ incorrect

b. bug – frog – cat ☐ correct ☐ incorrect   e. net – five – coat ☐ correct ☐ incorrect

c. drum – pig – worm ☐ correct ☐ incorrect   f. top – sheep – bird ☐ correct ☐ incorrect

Subtotal ☐ correct ☐ incorrect

6. Isolating Final Phonemes

Listen carefully. I am going to say a word. I would like you to tell me the ending sound of the word. If I said, *"dog,"* you would say /g/. *(Model more examples if the student looks unsure.)* Repeat each word and then say the last sound.

a. crab /b/ ☐ correct ☐ incorrect   e. pail /l/ ☐ correct ☐ incorrect

b. bird /d/ ☐ correct ☐ incorrect   f. ran /n/ ☐ correct ☐ incorrect

c. rug /g/ ☐ correct ☐ incorrect   g. broom /m/ ☐ correct ☐ incorrect

d. clock /k/ ☐ correct ☐ incorrect   h. boat /t/ ☐ correct ☐ incorrect

Subtotal ☐ correct ☐ incorrect

7. Blending Phonemes

Listen carefully. I am going to say some sounds and you are going to put the sounds together to make a word. For example, if I say /b/ /i/ /g/, the word would be *big. (Model more examples if the student looks unsure.)* Are you ready? I will say the sounds and then you say the word.

a. run ☐ correct ☐ incorrect   e. sock ☐ correct ☐ incorrect

b. sit ☐ correct ☐ incorrect   f. ball ☐ correct ☐ incorrect

c. fan ☐ correct ☐ incorrect   g. hand ☐ correct ☐ incorrect

d. dish ☐ correct ☐ incorrect   h. jump ☐ correct ☐ incorrect

Subtotal ☐ correct ☐ incorrect

8. Segmenting Phonemes

Listen carefully. This time I am going to say a word and you are going to break the word apart. For example, if I say *dog,* you would say /d/ /o/ /g/. *(Model more examples if the student looks unsure.)* Are you ready? I will say the words and then you say the sounds.

a. /c/ /a/ /t/ ☐ correct ☐ incorrect   e. /ch/ /i/ /p/ ☐ correct ☐ incorrect

b. /f/ /i/ /sh/ ☐ correct ☐ incorrect   f. /t/ /u/ /b/ ☐ correct ☐ incorrect

c. /m/ /a/ /n/ ☐ correct ☐ incorrect   g. /b/ /e/ /ll/ ☐ correct ☐ incorrect

d. /r/ /e/ /d/ ☐ correct ☐ incorrect   h. /s/ /o/ /ck/ ☐ correct ☐ incorrect

Subtotal ☐ correct ☐ incorrect

Subtotal ☐ correct ☐ incorrect

9. Manipulating Phonemes

(This is by far the most difficult section because it deals with skills that are not usually mastered until after kindergarten.) Listen carefully. I am going to say a word and then ask you to make a new word. For example, if I said, *"rain"* and asked you to add a /t/, you would say *"train."* If I said, *"blast"* and asked you to take way the /b/, you would say *"last."* If I said *"cot"* and asked you to change the /c/ to /d/, you would say *"dot." (Model more examples if the student looks unsure.).*

a. lap, add a /c/ (clap) ☐ correct ☐ incorrect   e. candy, take away /k/ (Andy) ☐ correct ☐ incorrect

b. ear, add a /t/ (tear) ☐ correct ☐ incorrect   f. hat, change the /h/ to /s/ (sat) ☐ correct ☐ incorrect

c. lock, add a /k/ (clock) ☐ correct ☐ incorrect   g. lake, change the /l/ to /r/ (rake) ☐ correct ☐ incorrect

d. skid, take away /s/ (kid) ☐ correct ☐ incorrect   h. hen, change the /h/ to /p/ (pen) ☐ correct ☐ incorrect

Subtotal ☐ correct ☐ incorrect

Total for Assessment ☐ correct ☐ incorrect

Chapter 3
RAPID AUTOMATIC NAMING (RAN)

What Is Rapid Automatic Naming?

Rapid automatic naming (RAN) is considered to be an integral part of reading and is highly correlated with success in reading. RAN is demonstrated by first learning the name of something and then being able to recognize it and then name it quickly—automatically.

As discussed in the Introduction on pages 5 and 6, *Developing Early Literacy: Report of the National Early Literacy Panel* (2009) identified the early skills that are the precursors of later literacy development. Of the six skills found to be predictive of later achievement, two of those skills are:

◆ Rapid automatic naming (RAN) of letters or digits: the ability to rapidly name a sequence of random letters or digits

◆ Rapid automatic naming (RAN) of objects or colors: the ability to rapidly name a sequence of repeating random sets of pictures of objects (e.g., "car," "tree," "house," "man") or colors

Why Is RAN Important?

Reading research has established that a student's ability to read is greatly influenced by the development of phonological processing skills. It is also known that fluency and reading accuracy are affected by a student's ability to recognize and quickly name a letter or cluster of letters. It seems obvious that recognizing the sounds and written symbols of language is imperative to being able to read. It does not seem as obvious as to why the skill of rapidly and automatically naming letters is so important to fluency and reading accuracy (which leads to reading success).

Letters are the building blocks of words. Naturally, young readers will encounter words with letters that they do not see frequently. For example, the letters *a* and *t* are seen in many more words than the letters *q* and *x*. Words that contain infrequently used letters can interfere with a student's fluency, which then decreases a student's reading comprehension.

Automatic letter recognition is the key to automatic word recognition. Unfortunately, this can be extremely challenging for many children. Dr. Virginia Berninger, professor at the University of Washington, found that at-risk students need 20 times more practice with literacy skills than the students who were not deemed at risk.

All students must overlearn letter recognition so that a *q* is as familiar as an *a*. Young students must learn to identify each letter shape and associate the shapes of each letter with its name and sound. This overlearning will lead to improved fluency, reading accuracy, and comprehension.

RAPID AUTOMATIC NAMING (RAN)

What Can Teachers Do to Improve Students' RAN Abilities?

Teachers are finding a number of clever intervention strategies and activities that can help students improve their abilities to automatically recognize and name objects, colors, numbers, letters, and words, as well as help students remember and say their addresses and phone numbers.

RAN Boards—Pages 103–116

Many teachers are finding "**RAN boards**" effective. A RAN board is simply a sheet of paper where the teacher has drawn a bingo- or lotto-like grid. Each box on the grid contains something that the student is currently working on. For example, if a student is learning to recognize the printed letters of his name, the teacher would first teach the shape of each letter using manipulatives or tactile activities. Next, the teacher would teach the student how to spell his name out loud. Then, the teacher would write the letters of the student's name in the boxes on the RAN board (*see illustration*). The student would point to each letter and say its name. If he forgets a letter, the student can spell his name aloud which often helps a student visually identify the forgotten letter.

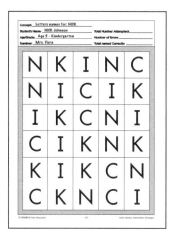

Generally, when using RAN boards with young students who are prereaders, it is a good idea to begin with naming objects, animals, and pictures of people and then move to colors, shapes, numbers, letters, and, eventually, words. See the reproducible RAN boards provided below and on pages 104–116. For RAN boards to be the most effective, they should be designed specifically for individual students.

Name RAN Boards Use directions from above.

✂

Concept: _**Letters in Name**_	
Student's Name: _____	Total Number Attempted: _____
Age/Grade: _____	Number of Errors: _____
Examiner: _____	Total Named Correctly: _____

How Fast Can You Say Your Address?

Directions: Print the child's address on the side of the mailbox. Have the child recite the address while pointing to each number, letter, or word.

How Fast Can You Say Your Phone Number?

Directions: Print the child's phone number on the phone. Have the child recite the phone number while pointing to each number.

Concept: **Farm Animals**

Student's Name: _____

Age/Grade: _____

Examiner: _____

Total Number Attempted: _____

Number of Errors: _____

Total Named Correctly: _____

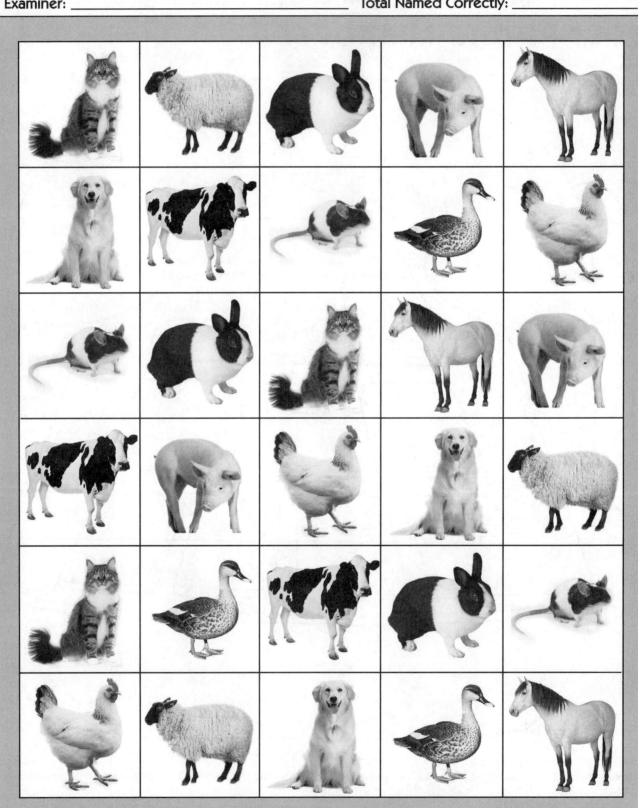

Concept: **Objects**

Student's Name: _____

Age/Grade: _____

Examiner: _____

Total Number Attempted: _____

Number of Errors: _____

Total Named Correctly: _____

- 107 - *Early Literacy Intervention Activities*

Concept: __Colors__

Student's Name: _____

Age/Grade: _____

Examiner: _____

Total Number Attempted: _____

Number of Errors: _____

Total Named Correctly: _____

Color this square **red**	Color this square **green**	Color this square **brown**	Color this square **blue**	Color this square **black**
Color this square **pink**	Color this square **white**	Color this square **yellow**	Color this square **orange**	Color this square **purple**
Color this square **blue**	Color this square **brown**	Color this square **red**	Color this square **green**	Color this square **yellow**
Color this square **black**	Color this square **green**	Color this square **purple**	Color this square **red**	Color this square **orange**
Color this square **white**	Color this square **blue**	Color this square **orange**	Color this square **black**	Color this square **pink**
Color this square **pink**	Color this square **brown**	Color this square **yellow**	Color this square **white**	Color this square **purple**

Concept: **Numbers 0 to 10**

Reproducible RAN Boards
(Directions are found on page 103.)

Student's Name: _____

Age/Grade: _____

Examiner: _____

Total Number Attempted: _____

Number of Errors: _____

Total Named Correctly: _____

10	7	5	2	1
1	9	4	8	9
8	2	6	0	3
4	2	5	7	10
7	8	3	6	4
6	0	9	5	1

Concept: **6 Letters—A through F**

Reproducible RAN Boards
(Directions are found on page 103.)

Student's Name: _____

Total Number Attempted: _____

Age/Grade: _____

Number of Errors: _____

Examiner: _____

Total Named Correctly: _____

A	C	E	D	B
E	B	D	F	D
F	C	A	E	A
D	A	D	C	F
B	E	F	A	B
C	D	C	F	B

Student's Name: _____

Total Number Attempted: _____

Age/Grade: _____

Number of Errors: _____

Examiner: _____

Total Named Correctly: _____

G	K	I	H	L
L	K	J	I	K
G	I	H	J	G
J	K	I	H	L
K	L	G	J	H
G	H	L	I	J

Student's Name: _____

Age/Grade: _____

Examiner: _____

Total Number Attempted: _____

Number of Errors: _____

Total Named Correctly: _____

M	S	P	R	S
S	N	Q	M	N
M	S	O	R	P
Q	N	R	P	M
R	O	P	O	Q
O	Q	N	R	M

Concept: 7 Letters—T through Z

Reproducible RAN Boards
(Directions are found on page 103.)

Student's Name: ______________________ Total Number Attempted: ______________

Age/Grade: ______________________ Number of Errors: ______________

Examiner: ______________________ Total Named Correctly: ______________

T	Y	Z	W	U
X	V	Y	U	Z
W	U	Y	V	T
Z	T	W	Y	V
T	W	X	Z	X
V	Y	U	T	W

Concept: **Alphabet—Uppercase**

Reproducible RAN Boards
(Directions are found on page 103.)

Student's Name: ______________________ Total Number Attempted: __________

Age/Grade: ______________________ Number of Errors: __________

Examiner: ______________________ Total Named Correctly: __________

A	U	N	S	K
Q	E	H	D	W
J	M	B	Y	O
V	Z	R	T	F

P	C	I	X	G	L

Concept: **Alphabet—Lowercase**

Reproducible RAN Boards
(Directions are found on page 103.)

Student's Name: _____

Total Number Attempted: _____

Age/Grade: _____

Number of Errors: _____

Examiner: _____

Total Named Correctly: _____

t	e	x	j	o
d	s	a	r	h
p	k	l	b	n
w	c	v	g	q
m	z	i	y	f	u

Concept:_____

Student's Name:_____

Age/Grade:_____

Examiner:_____

Total Number Attempted:_____

Number of Errors:_____

Total Named Correctly:_____

Chapter 4
WRITING NAMES & LETTERS & EARLY WRITING EXPERIENCES

Another strong predictor of reading success is the ability to write letters in isolation upon request or to write one's own name. This chapter will provide some effective strategies to help young children learn how to write their own names and learn how to print letters using a developmental approach. It also offers teaching suggestions and intervention strategies to enrich early writing experiences.

The Predictable Path of Learning How to Write

Children go through developmental stages of learning how to write. When a teacher understands the stage where each of her students is, she can then target instruction to meet the student's specific needs. The stages of writing are best described as behaviors.

Prewriters

◆ **Scribbling:** At first, the child scribbles exclusively. There is little pencil control, and the child may not even be able to describe what is being scribbled. Eventually, the paper will have pictures and scribbles and the child will be able to tell you what the pictures are about.

◆ **Zigzag Writing:** Next, the child begins to create shapes and then letterlike symbols. These symbols may be drawings that look similar to letters or up-and-down zigzag writing.

Early Writers

◆ **Writing—"Talk" Written Down:** At this stage, children understand that writing represents thoughts and conveys messages.

◆ **Random Letters and Pictures:** The child may write one letter, often an initial consonant, to represent a word. Children may also show some beginning letter-to-sound correspondence as well as the ability to "read" their own "writing."

◆ **Choosing topics:** During this stage, children may choose their own writing topics.

Emergent Writers

◆ **Stories and Pictures Match:** Students are now able to draw pictures that match the stories they are trying to write.

◆ **Writing with Invented Spelling:** Random letters and scribbling is now replaced with "words." Any words the child does not know how to spell will be created phonetically using invented spelling.

◆ **Real Words:** During this stage students may also copy words from word walls or print high-frequency words, along with random use of punctuation.

Modes of Writing

Although individual and small group instruction is the most effective, that is not always possible. There are both large and small group activities that can successfully enhance a student's developing writing skills.

Language Experience Writing

This form of writing has been used effectively by teachers for many years. Language experience writing draws upon the students' experiences, such as what happened on a field trip or what happened that day on the playground. The teacher acts as a scribe and writes down exactly what the students say about a topic. The students then reread the script together giving the teacher an opportunity to demonstrate word spacing, directionality, and return sweep. A language experience story is also a good way to help build vocabulary.

WRITING NAMES & LETTERS & EARLY WRITING EXPERIENCES

Shared Writing

Shared writing occurs when the teacher and students work together to compose a text. The teacher takes the lead role and guides the process by thinking aloud and by demonstrating how people write down their thoughts. The teacher can also draw attention to concepts of print, model writing strategies, and provide an opportunity to change and manipulate the text as the students contribute to the writing process.

These are some questions that you can use during a shared writing activity.

1. Who has an idea for what we could write about?
2. What should we use to write with?
3. Where should we begin to write?
4. What do you think about . . . ?
5. Who else would like to add something?
6. Do I need a period here?
7. Is this a question? What do I need if it is a question?
8. Is there enough space between these words?
9. What letter does this word begin with?

Interactive Writing

Interactive writing allows students to take a more active role in the writing process. Interactive writing begins in kindergarten and incorporates many of the shared reading strategies as well as allows children to actually share the pencil and write!

Consider these points as you guide your students through an interactive writing activity:

- alliteration
- blending
- curriculum connections
- directionality
- grammar
- letter form
- letter identification
- one-to-one correspondence
- punctuation
- return sweep
- rhyming
- segmenting
- sound-letter relationships
- spacing
- upper- and lowercase letters
- vocabulary development

The Beginning—Learning How to Write One's Own Name

For many young children, learning how to read and write their own names is exciting and helps them feel a little more grown-up. Here are lots of ideas to motivate young writers.

Daily Sign-In Boards

Use chart paper with the caption, "Who is here today?" When the children come in, they can sign their names on the paper. At the beginning of the year, you or an adult room helper can assist the students. During morning circle time, the class can read all of the names together.

Vary the type of sign-in board you use as well as the writing utensils to keep the daily name-writing task interesting. Write on a white board, poster board, a blackboard, index cards, or newsprint with finger paint, colored markers, chalk, glitter pens, and so on.

Laminated Write On/Wipe Off Name Cards—Page 138

Use the reproducible Blank Writing Line Template found on page 138. On the top line, print the child's name, either very lightly or use dotted letters (see illustration). Then, laminate the page to create a write on/wipe off name card. Students can practice tracing their names with crayons, wipe them off, and begin again. Use a full page for students who enjoy writing practice; for students who find learning to print a frustrating experience, cut the page in two to make half-page name cards.

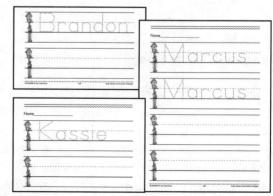

WRITING NAMES & LETTERS & EARLY WRITING EXPERIENCES

Name Wall

Use a concept similar to a word wall for having children sign in. Print the initial letter of each student's first name on the chalkboard or on a large piece of paper. Have the students find the first letters of their names and write the remaining letters to finish their names.

My Autograph Book

Create an autograph book for each child by folding several sheets of copy paper in half. Then, fold a piece of card stock in half. Slip the card stock over the copy paper to create a cover for the autograph book and staple it along the fold. Write "My Autograph Book" on the cover and leave a space for the child's name. Invite children to decorate their covers with stickers, drawings, etc.

Create a Classroom Writing Center

A writing center is an important activity center in a preschool or kindergarten classroom. This center should be designed to encourage young children to want to explore and experiment with writing and various writing materials. Remember to keep your center interesting by changing the supplies on a regular basis.

Materials for a Writing Center

Paper	Writing Tools	Other Supplies
◆ adding machine tape	◆ chalk	◆ books and pictures to use as springboards for writing
◆ blank & lined paper	◆ colored pencils	◆ clay or play dough
◆ blank books	◆ crayons	◆ clipboards
◆ cardboard	◆ erasers	◆ computer (word processing program)
◆ card stock	◆ markers	◆ dictionaries (words and pictures)
◆ construction paper	◆ paint	◆ glue
◆ envelopes	◆ paintbrushes	◆ letter cookie cutters
◆ finger painting paper	◆ pencil grips	◆ magic slates
◆ greeting cards	◆ pencils	◆ typewriter
◆ index cards	◆ pens	◆ paper clips
◆ journals		◆ sand or salt tray
◆ newsprint		◆ stamps and ink pads
◆ postcards		◆ stencils (shape and letters)
◆ stationery		◆ stickers
◆ textured paper		◆ tape
◆ wallpaper		

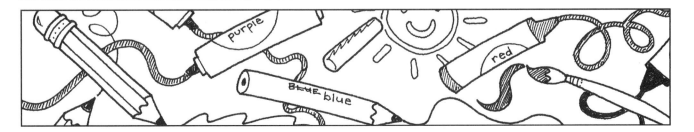

WRITING NAMES & LETTERS & EARLY WRITING EXPERIENCES

List Writing

Lists are a great first writing assignment. They require no grammar and little formatting and can be used later on to generate writing ideas. Brainstorming is really just a list, no matter what form it takes. For the class's first writing lessons, find time each day for students to make different lists using the following writing activities and reproducibles. Allow students to read their lists aloud when possible. Students with special needs and beginning writers may need to type or dictate their answers.

Here are some writing suggestions for lists:

- animals
- body parts
- clothing
- colors and shapes
- days and months
- dinosaurs
- favorite books/stories
- favorite foods
- favorite things
- favorite toys
- furniture
- games
- ingredients in a recipe
- names of family
- names of friends
- outside activities
- sports
- weather

Cut-Up Sentences

The hands-on reading activity of assembling "cut-up" or mixed-up sentences is a strategy that has been well documented as an effective tool for teaching young children how to read and write. This approach is currently being utilized by a wide variety of reading philosophies and practices. It has been integrated into many of the most prominent basal reading programs and is considered an essential activity in the prescribed lessons of the Reading Recovery® program and in the Four-Blocks® Literacy Model.

Write simple, incomplete sentences on sentence strips. The children can cut out and glue the first words of the sentences and then finish the sentences by writing a word or drawing a picture. Here are some examples:

- I am _____.
- I can _____ the _____.
- I like the _____.
- Look at the _____.
- I see a _____.
- I feel _____.
- My house has a _____.
- I like to play _____.
- This is a _____.
- Here comes a _____.
- I see my _____.
- I like _____.
- I like my _____.
- Here is a _____.
- Let's go to the _____.

Journaling—Page 121

Provide children with various journal prompts to get them started writing. Add positive comments to what the children have written. Remember, the purpose of journal writing is to provide meaningful writing practice on topics that interest and motivate young writers. Copy page 121 to make large journals for students. Children might also enjoy writing in six-page mini-journals created from one sheet of paper.

Six-Page Mini-Journal

1. Fold a letter- or legal-sized piece of paper in half lengthwise (like a hot dog) to make a doubled strip.
2. Fold the strip in half vertically.
3. With the vertical fold on the left, fold the right edge (the paper is doubled) toward the vertical fold.
4. Turn the paper over and also fold the other doubled edge toward the vertical fold.
5. Staple the two folded edges together as shown to create the six-page mini-journal.

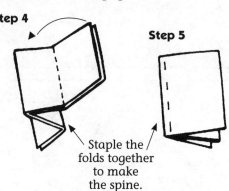

Step 4

Step 5

Staple the folds together to make the spine.

MY JOURNAL

DEVELOPMENTAL APPROACH TO WRITING LETTERS

There are nine handwriting strokes to master in order to learn to print (*see below*). As these strokes are practiced, children will also be learning how to print individual alphabet letters. After children have learned how to make tall and long straight line strokes, they will be able to print nine letters: *l, i, L, T, t, F, E, H,* and *I*. Next, the children will learn tall slanted strokes and will be able to print another nine letters: *V, W, N, M, Z, X, A, Y,* and *K*. Then, they will learn small slanted strokes, which will add six more letters: *v, w, z, x, y,* and *k*. At this point, the children will be printing 24 of the 52 letters.

Next, the children will learn circles and will print the letters *O, Q,* and *o*. Some of the more difficult letters will be introduced next as they learn the left-ear curve stroke and eight letters: *C, G, c, a, e, d, g,* and *q*. These are followed by learning the right-ear curve stroke and six more letters: *D, P, B, R, b,* and *p*. Now, the children can print 41 of the 52 letters. The letters *S* and *s* are taught individually because these letters are actually a combination of a left-ear and a right-ear curve. Children have reached the last two strokes as they learn the smiling curve and the letters *U, J, u,* and *j*, and the frowning curve and the letters *n, m, h, r,* and *f*. Now, the children will have successfully learned how to print all of the lowercase and uppercase alphabet letters!

The Nine Strokes Necessary for Learning to Print

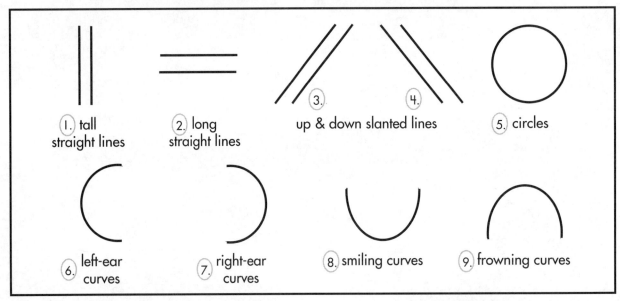

1. tall straight lines
2. long straight lines
3. 4. up & down slanted lines
5. circles
6. left-ear curves
7. right-ear curves
8. smiling curves
9. frowning curves

(Copy, cut out, and laminate the Individual Student Desk Chart for each student. Tape the chart to the student's desk for a reference tool or for motivation. Each time the printing of a letter is mastered, the student can color that letter on the chart.)

Name: _____   **Individual Student Desk Chart**

tall & long straight lines	tall slanted lines
l i L T t F E H I	V W N M

tall slanted lines cont.	small slanted lines	circles
Z X A Y K	v w z x y k	O Q

circles	left-ear curves	right-ear curves
o	C G c a e d g q	D P B R

right-ear curves cont.	left & right ear curves	smiling curves	frowning curves
b p	S s	U J u j	n m h r f

Student Checklist

Name_____ **Date** _____

1. Student has mastered the following nine strokes necessary for learning how to print:

- ❑ tall straight lines
- ❑ long straight lines
- ❑ slanted up lines
- ❑ slanted down lines
- ❑ circles
- ❑ left-ear curves
- ❑ right-ear curves
- ❑ smiling curves
- ❑ frowning curves

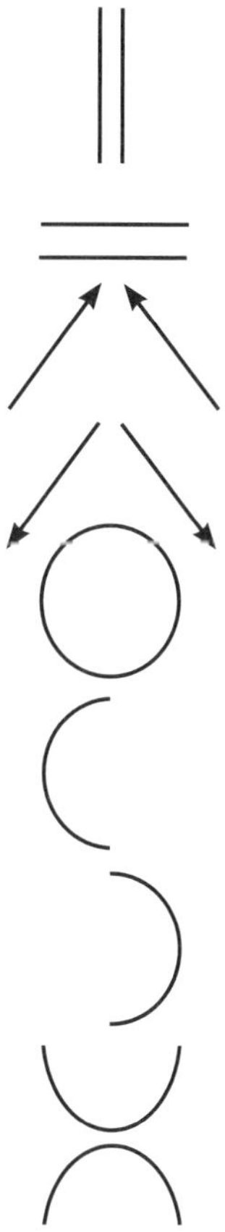

2. Student has mastered the ability to draw the following shapes:

- ❑ square
- ❑ rectangle
- ❑ triangle
- ❑ rhombus
- ❑ circle
- ❑ oval

3. Student is able to print the following letters:

tall and long straight lines
- ❑ I
- ❑ i
- ❑ L
- ❑ T
- ❑ t
- ❑ F
- ❑ E
- ❑ H
- ❑ l

slanted lines
- ❑ V
- ❑ v
- ❑ W
- ❑ w
- ❑ N
- ❑ M
- ❑ Z
- ❑ z
- ❑ X
- ❑ x
- ❑ A
- ❑ Y
- ❑ y
- ❑ K
- ❑ k

circles
- ❑ O
- ❑ o
- ❑ Q

left-ear curves
- ❑ C
- ❑ c
- ❑ G
- ❑ e
- ❑ a
- ❑ d
- ❑ g
- ❑ q

right-ear curves
- ❑ D
- ❑ P
- ❑ p
- ❑ B
- ❑ b
- ❑ R

left- and right-ear curves
- ❑ S
- ❑ s

smiling curves
- ❑ U
- ❑ u
- ❑ J
- ❑ j

frowning curves
- ❑ n
- ❑ m
- ❑ r
- ❑ h
- ❑ f

LEARN ABOUT GUIDE LINES

The reproducible Blank Writing Line Template on page 138 features a birdhouse at the beginning of each line. This is to help guide the children in learning and remembering how each letter is formed. Use the birdhouse to tell a story about each letter. For example, when making a lowercase *l*, you can say, "Start drawing at the top line (or at the top of the birdhouse). Then, bring the line down until it touches the grass."

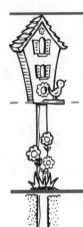

This is the top line or the top of the birdhouse.

This is the middle line or the dashed line where the bird sits.

This is the bottom line or the line where there is grass.

This is below the bottom line or "underground."
Letter tails may go underground and touch the worm.

Here are some examples:

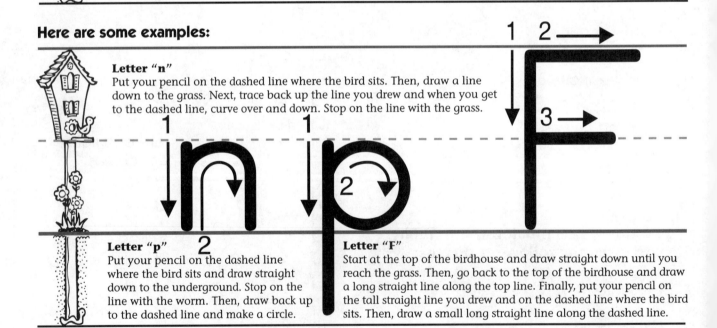

Letter "n"
Put your pencil on the dashed line where the bird sits. Then, draw a line down to the grass. Next, trace back up the line you drew and when you get to the dashed line, curve over and down. Stop on the line with the grass.

Letter "p"
Put your pencil on the dashed line where the bird sits and draw straight down to the underground. Stop on the line with the worm. Then, draw back up to the dashed line and make a circle.

Letter "F"
Start at the top of the birdhouse and draw straight down until you reach the grass. Then, go back to the top of the birdhouse and draw a long straight line along the top line. Finally, put your pencil on the tall straight line you drew and on the dashed line where the bird sits. Then, draw a small long straight line along the dashed line.

Reproducible "Tactile Touch & Trace" Printing Cards—Pages 125–137

To aid in the developmental process of learning how to print, use the "Tactile Touch & Trace" printing cards found on pages 125–137. Reproduce these cards onto card stock and cut out along the dotted lines. Trace over each letter with glitter glue, puff paint, or a craft glue. Allow to dry. The children will be able to trace the letters with their fingers and "feel" how each letter is formed. This tactile sensation will help imprint the correct direction of each letter stroke and help the child remember the proper letter formation. Use a touch and trace letter before each individual letter is introduced. Have each child make a personal set of Touch & Trace letter cards to take home for additional practice.

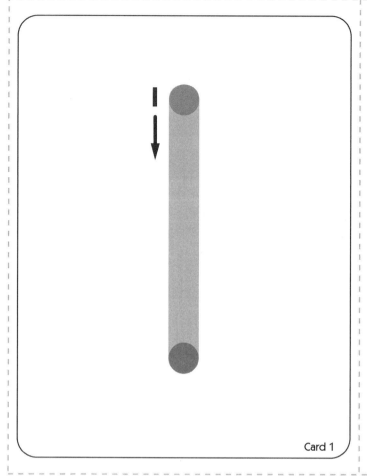

Card 1

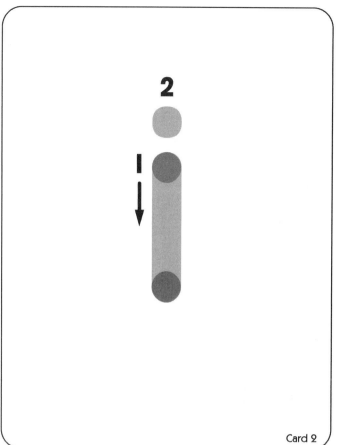

Card 2

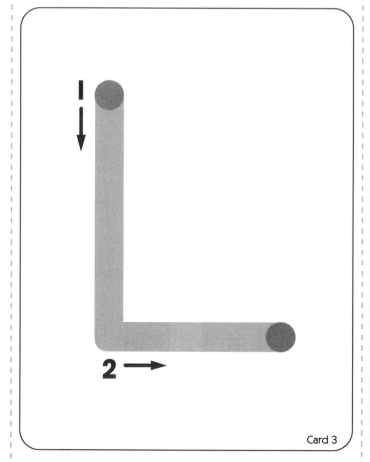

Card 3

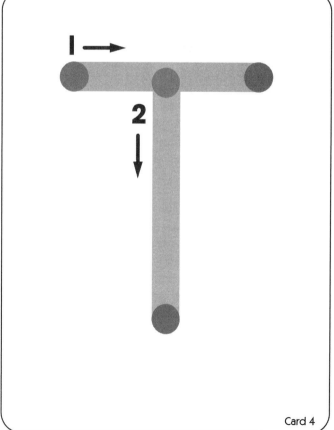

Card 4

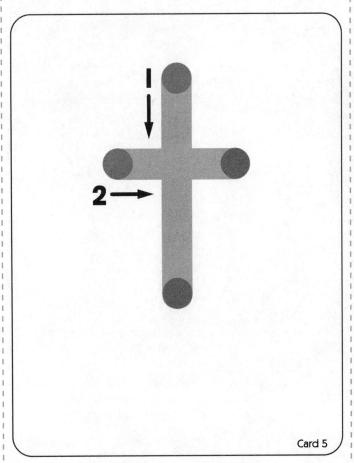

Card 5

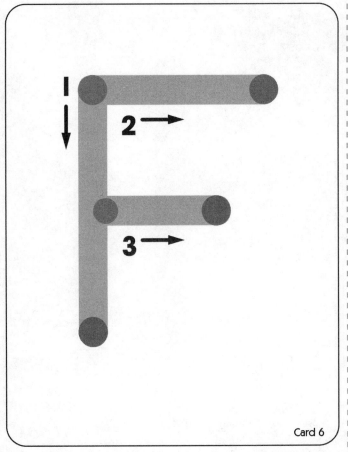

Card 6

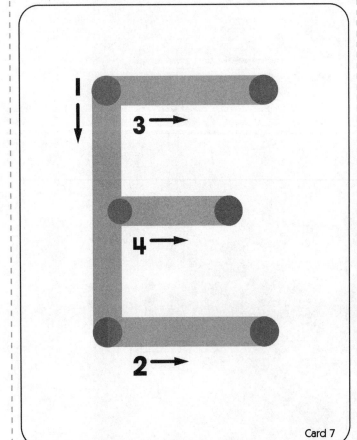

Card 7

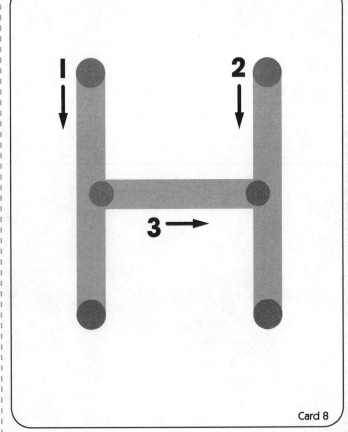

Card 8

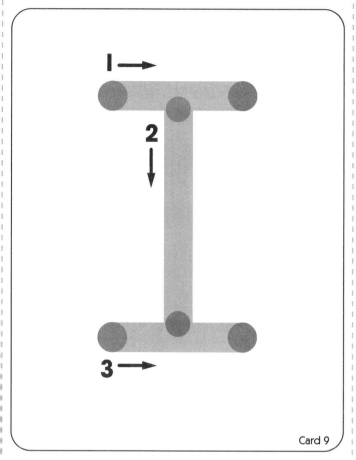

Card 9

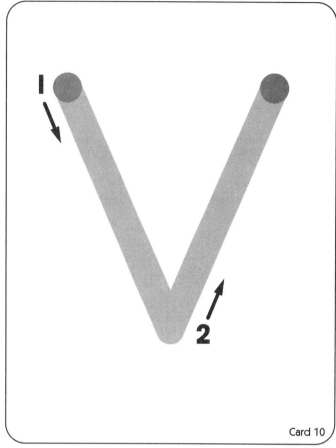

Card 10

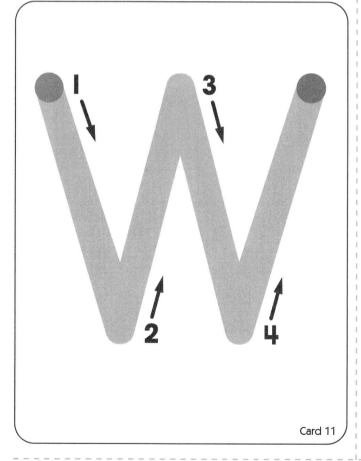

Card 11

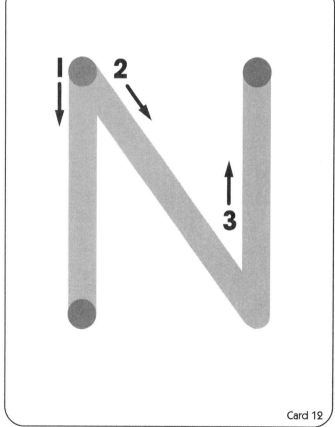

Card 12

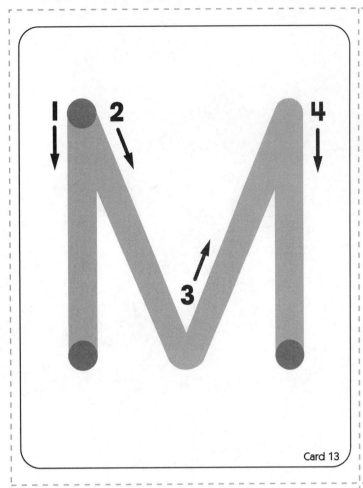

Card 13

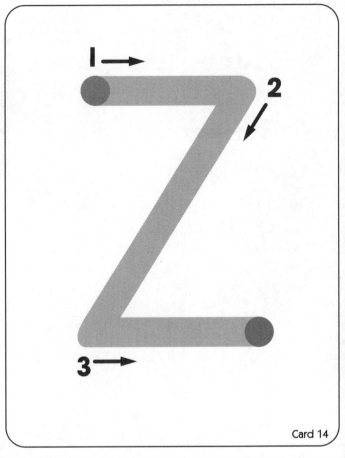

Card 14

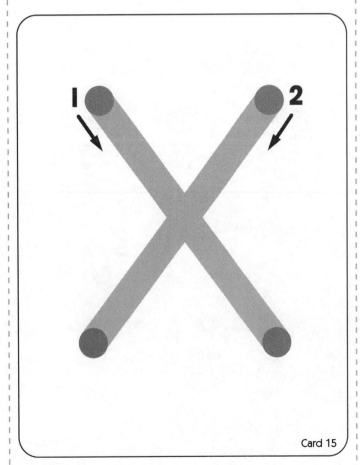

Card 15

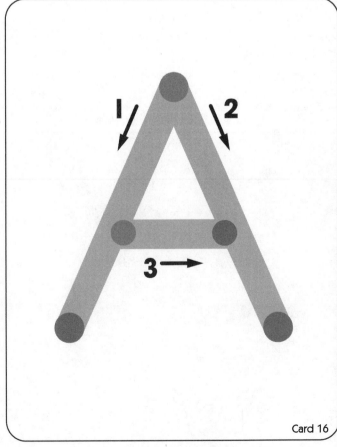

Card 16

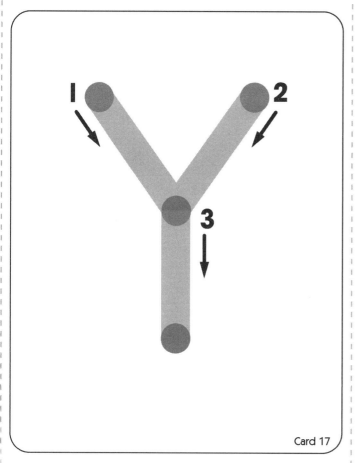

Card 17

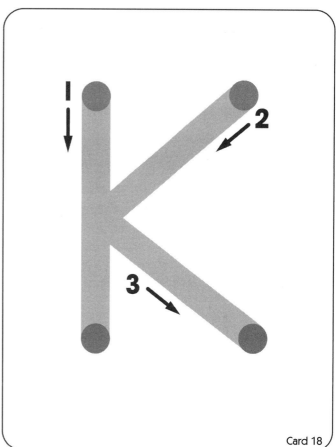

Card 18

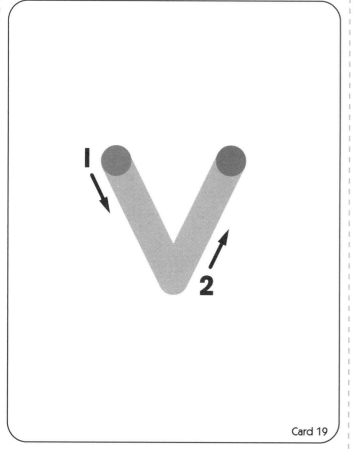

Card 19

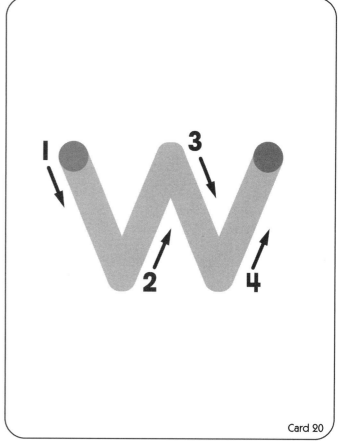

Card 20

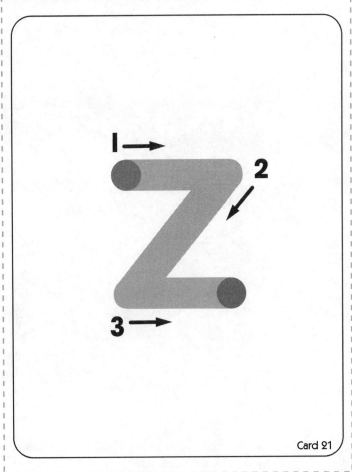

Card 21

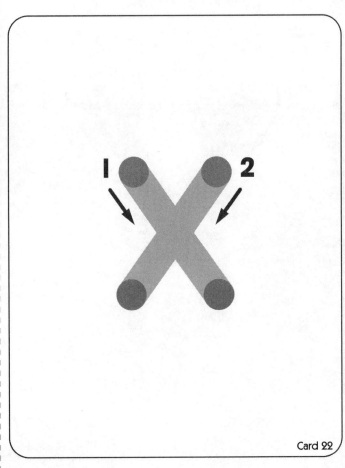

Card 22

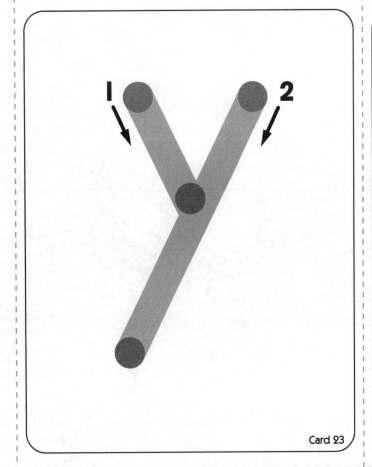

Card 23

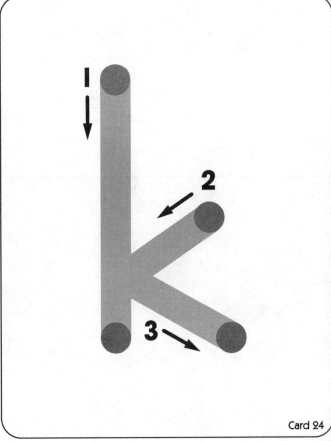

Card 24

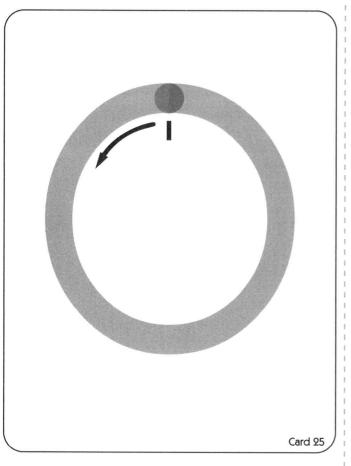

Card 25

Card 26

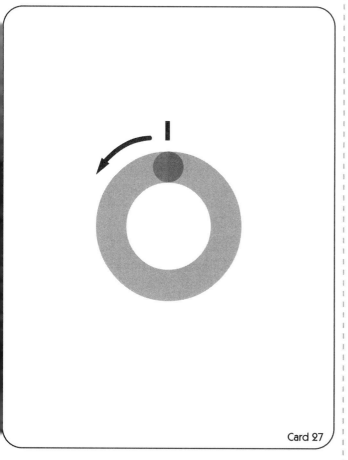

Card 27

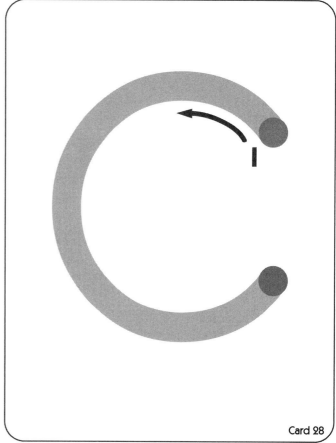

Card 28

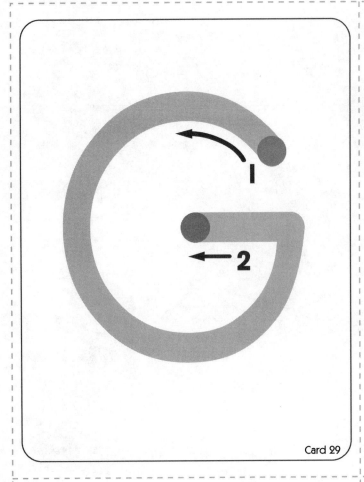

Card 29

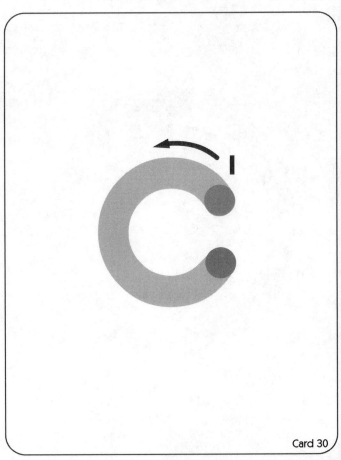

Card 30

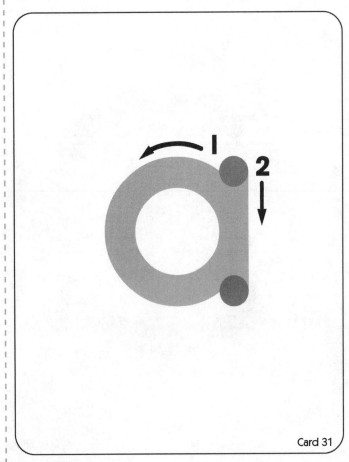

Card 31

Card 32

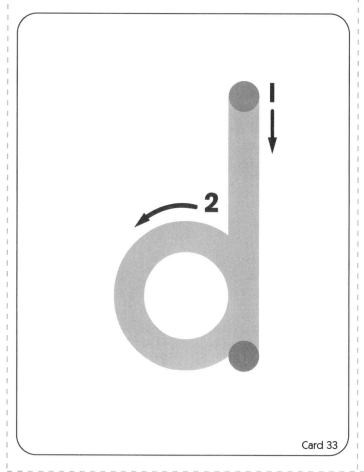

Card 33

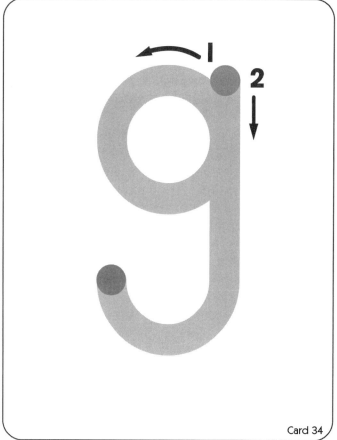

Card 34

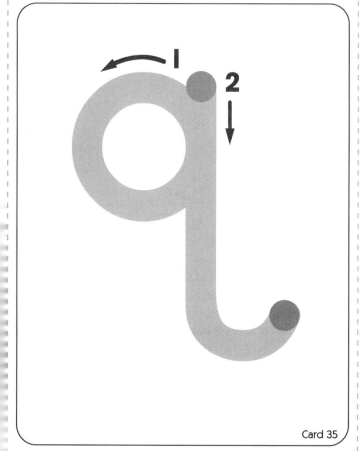

Card 35

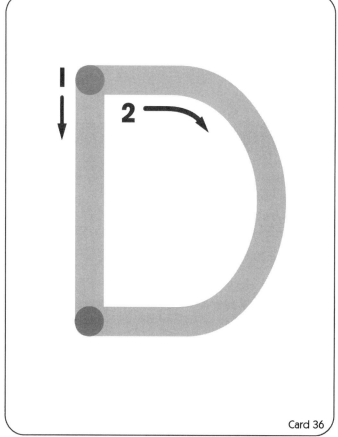

Card 36

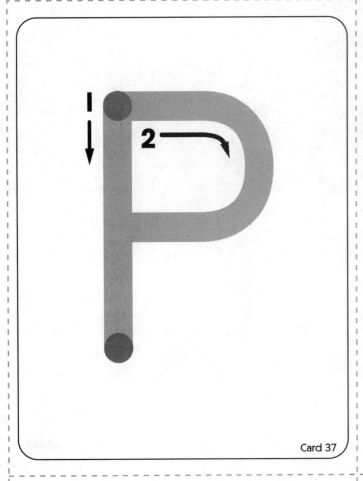

Card 37

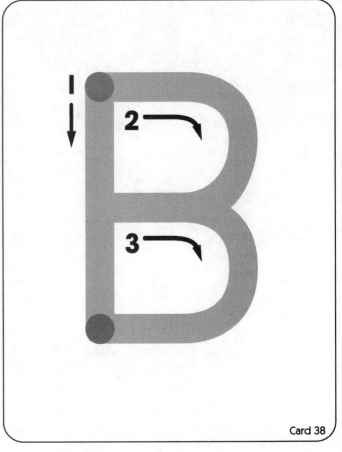

Card 38

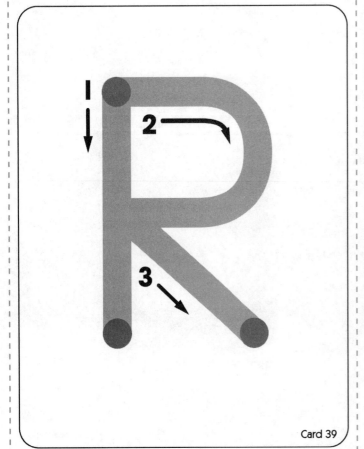

Card 39

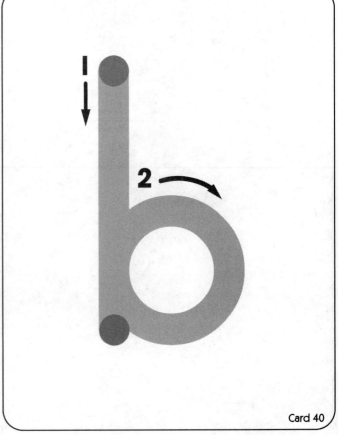

Card 40

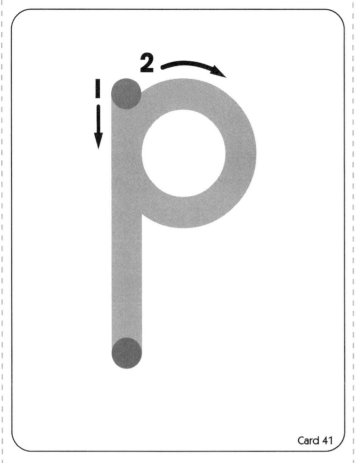

Card 41

Card 42

Card 43

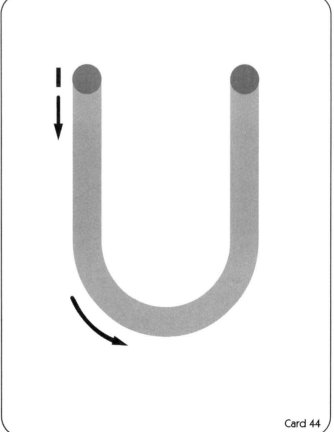

Card 44

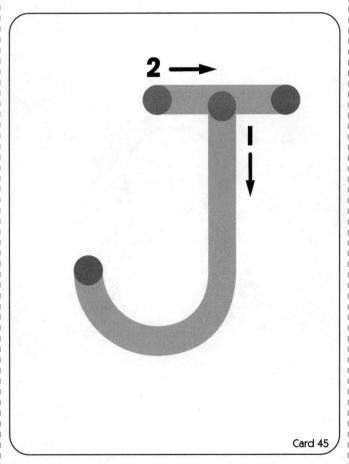

Card 45

Card 46

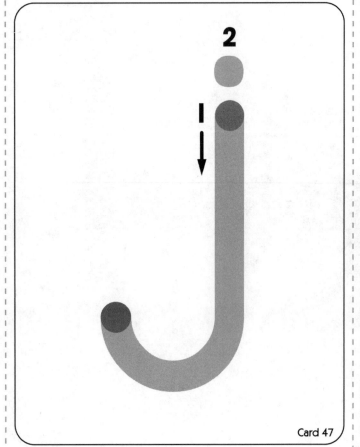

Card 47

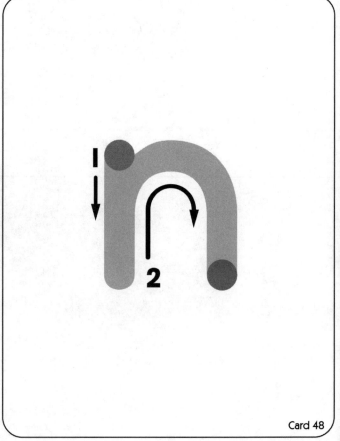

Card 48

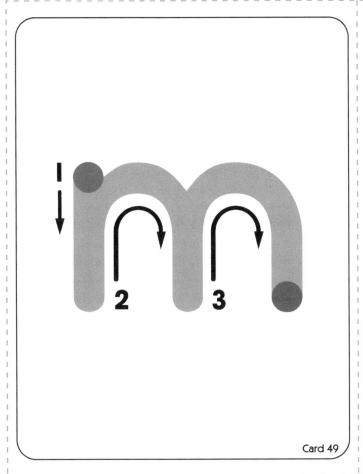

Card 49

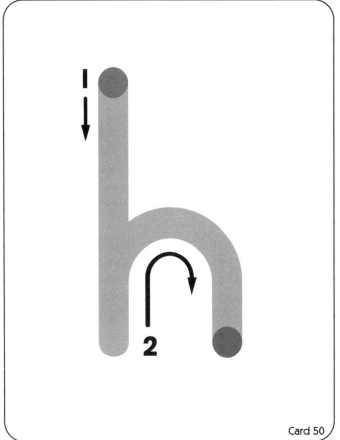

Card 50

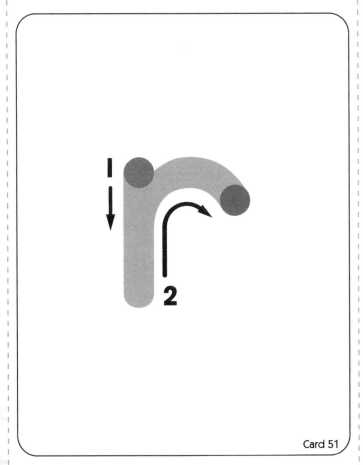

Card 51

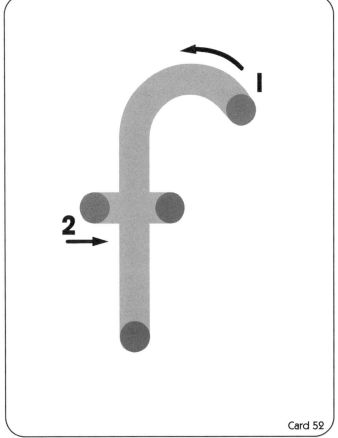

Card 52

Name_____

Blank Writing Line Template

Chapter 5

PHONOLOGICAL MEMORY

What Is Phonological Memory?

As was discussed in the Introduction, the wealth of early literacy research shows that some early literacy skills appear to be more important than others. To review, the strongest and most consistent predictors of later literacy achievement are alphabet knowledge, phonological awareness, phonological memory, rapid automatized naming, and writing letters. This chapter will focus on probably the least understood predictor—phonological memory.

> **Phonological memory is the ability to remember spoken information for a short period of time.**

Phonological memory is the skill that helps children to remember simple, multistep instructions such as following directions when picking up toys, standing in line to go out to play, or getting things ready for school in the morning. Phonological memory also helps children in remembering the beginning part of a story read aloud so that the ending of the story will make sense. Phonological memory, sometimes referred to as phonological working memory, also plays a significant role in distinguishing and connecting speech sounds, as well as recognizing speech and letter correspondence—crucial tasks during the first stages of learning how to read.

As described in Chapter 2, phonological awareness is a phonological processing skill that is important to early decoding (word attack skills). In addition to phonological awareness, the contributions of phonological working memory to early decoding have been well established for children who are progressing as expected as well as for children with reading disorders or those with language difficulties. Researchers measured phonological working memory with repetition and span tasks—both word and nonword. The nonword recall tasks are believed to better demonstrate phonological working memory because they do not rely on a child's understanding of language and the meanings of words.

What Does the Current Research Say?

Thus far there has only been one study designed to answer the question: Can training of phonological memory contribute to reading development? The study involved 120 Greek-speaking kindergartners who were assigned randomly to a control or treatment group (Maridaki-Kassotaki 2002). This study trained children in nonword repetition in order to improve phonological working memory (and thus improve early literacy skills). The treatment lasted for the school year. On a reading test given at the end of first grade, the treatment group showed superior performance over the control group. This was only one study, but it does provide some evidence that training phonological memory with memory activities can benefit early reading skills.

In another study (Van Kleeck, Gillam, and Hoffman 2006) asked the question "Will training in phonological awareness generalize to phonological working memory?" Sixteen children with speech language impairments received 15 minutes of small-group lessons twice each week for two semesters. During the fall semester, children attended a **rhyming center** for 15 minutes two times per week. Children were led through a series of increasingly difficult rhyming activities. The activities progressed from recognition, to imitation, to identification, to judgment, and finally to rhyme creation.

During the spring semester, children attended a **phoneme awareness center** for 15 minutes two times per week. The children participated in activities to help them acquire an awareness of sounds at the beginning and end of words.

The children's performance on a series of phonological awareness tasks improved statistically, but so did their performance on two phonological working memory measures. In addition, the study found that children presented a larger improvement on the nonword recall task than on the single-syllable word recall task. The findings of this study provide evidence that using rhyming and phoneme awareness instruction resulted in improved phonological awareness and improved phonological working memory.

PHONOLOGICAL MEMORY: MEMORY BUILDING ACTIVITIES

Phonological Memory Building Strategies

As we saw in the research, there does seem to be some benefit to providing children with memory building activities. Use the suggestions and activities found in Chapter 2: Phonological Awareness (pages 64–101) to naturally assist in developing phonological working memory. Below are some additional memory building activities that can be effective and fun.

Repeat after Me

Read aloud a list of three or four words—only once—and then ask the children to repeat what they heard. Children will also have fun working in pairs, with one child reading (or saying) a list of words and the other child repeating it. The first child will have to listen carefully to discern whether the other child is repeating the list correctly. As a challenge activity, ask children to repeat the list backwards.

Environmental Sounds

At the end of the day, ask children to recall sounds that they heard throughout the day both in and out of the classroom, such as an airplane, a dog barking, the janitor talking in the hall, etc. See how many sounds the children remember hearing.

Fill in the Blanks

Read a familiar poem or rhyme. Then, read the rhyme again, only this time leave out some key words. Encourage children to verbally fill in the missing words. For example, say, "Old King _____, was a _____ old _____," or "Little Miss _____, sat on a _____, eating her _____ and _____."

Can You Do It?

Ask each child, one at a time, to do three things. Tell the children to listen carefully to all three things before performing the tasks. For example, say: 1. Stand up. 2. Jump two times. 3. Touch the top of your head. For some children, three tasks will be too many. Start with two tasks and, when you see that the children are ready for more, increase to three and then four tasks. For a variation, children will enjoy giving several simple directions to one another.

What Did You Hear?

Choose a detailed passage from a story to read aloud. Tell children to listen very carefully because you will ask them to do something when you have finished reading. After reading, give each of the children a blank piece of paper and some crayons. Then, have them draw a picture and include as many details from the passage as they can recall. When the children are finished drawing, read the passage again so that they can see how many things they remembered correctly. Let them add to their pictures the things they did not remember after the first reading of the passage.

Play Telephone

Playing the traditional game of telephone is actually an excellent activity for increasing auditory memory and for developing listening skills. Ask children to sit in a circle. Choose one child to whisper a sentence into the next child's ear. That child then whispers the same sentence to the next child and so on. Finally, when the sentence has gone the entire way around the circle, the last child says the sentence she heard out loud! More often than not, the sentence will have been altered in some way. The children will giggle with delight as they play this game, and they will become better listeners and develop stronger auditory memory skills.

Memorization Fun

Work together to help children memorize rhymes, songs, and tongue twisters and recite or sing them. Tape record, listen, and try to improve their recall skills for the next time you record.

Post a poem or rhyme on a bulletin board weekly. Challenge the class to see how many children can have it memorized by the end of the week.

Chapter 6

ORAL LANGUAGE

The Importance of Oral Language Skills

Researchers have found that oral language plays a major role in building the foundation for reading. Children who possess well-developed oral language skills are more likely to become successful readers (Snow Burns and Griffin 1998).

Oral language development includes the skills that allow children to communicate. Children develop **receptive language skills** as they listen and build their vocabularies and learn to understand a growing number of concepts that they have heard. Children also develop **expressive language skills** as they learn to express their own ideas, feelings, and thoughts using oral language.

Oral language development is a critical foundation for reading, writing, and spelling. Research suggests that young children's ability to use language and to listen to and understand the meaning of spoken words is related to their later literacy achievement. These oral language skills begin to develop in infancy and will continue to grow and expand throughout their lives.

What We Should Expect from Preschool and Kindergarten Children

By the time children arrive in kindergarten, most of them have a vocabulary of 3,000 to 5,000 words and are speaking in grammatically correct three- to four-word sentences. Unfortunately, there are many children who enter school with limited vocabularies. One study discovered that children living in poverty were exposed to half as many words by the age of three as their middle-class peers. When these children were evaluated again at age nine, the vocabulary gap was still evident: the children in poverty had not caught up with their classmates. We have also seen that word knowledge in preschool correlates to comprehension in the upper grades. So, it is critical that early childhood teachers "teach" vocabulary and develop strategies to build oral language skills.

Listening (Receptive Language Skills)

- Understands and follows simple directions
- Follows classroom routines
- Pays attention to the sounds in language (e.g., rhymes, alliteration, syllables, etc.)
- Enjoys listening to stories and can follow the sequence of the story
- Listens for a variety of purposes (e.g., to get information, to join in a conversation, to share a thought, etc.)

Speaking (Expressive Language Skills)

- Speaks in complete sentences
- Is beginning to speak using more complex sentence connectors (e.g., *if, or, when, because*, etc.)
- Knows how to take turns when speaking
- Speaks clearly and uses appropriate levels of inflection, volume, and tone
- Has a growing vocabulary and uses new words
- Asks questions
- Is able to ask for help when it is needed
- Initiates conversations with classmates and adults
- Expresses feelings and thoughts
- Relates experiences
- Recites or sings songs, rhymes, chants, and finger plays
- Tells and retells stories

ORAL LANGUAGE: SHARED CONVERSATIONS

The Importance of Conducting Meaningful and Purposeful Conversations with Children

One of the most effective strategies for increasing vocabulary development and language comprehension is having meaningful and purposeful conversations with young children. Language naturally builds upon itself—when children are regularly spoken to on a variety of interesting topics, they will become better at speaking and understanding. Both the quantity and quality of these exchanges are critical.

Here are some suggestions for creating a language-rich classroom and for encouraging high-quality conversations:

- Have conversations with young children on a regular basis
- Encourage children to extend conversations
- Have conversations about books, songs, stories, and personal experiences
- Encourage children to tell and retell stories
- Model the use of new vocabulary
- Discuss things that are of special interest to children
- Speak courteously to children and make eye contact at their level
- Ask questions that are open-ended
- Provide explicit feedback on vocabulary, word meaning, and pronunciation
- Show sincere interest in children and their thoughts
- Listen attentively to what each child has to say
- Use spontaneous opportunities to talk with each child individually
- Listen to what children are talking about and join in their conversations

---

Specific Suggestions for Shared Conversations

Children enjoy talking with the adults in their lives. Even a short conversation can help a child feel important. We all like to be heard. At the same time, while "conversing" with children, we can be explicitly teaching them ways to build and increase their oral language skills.

Take Turns While Talking. Good conversation involves two people talking. Model the back and forth of a conversation. Ask questions that will help the child extend the conversation. For example, if the child says, "I went to the pet store last night," ask, "What did you see at the pet store?" The child might reply, "I saw a dog." Respond, "Tell me about the dog. Was it little or big? What color was it?" and so on.

Have Individual Talking Time. Find some time during the day to have a conversation with every child in your class. Good times for this might be when children first arrive, on the playground, and during snack time and center times. Find moments for a good one-on-one conversation. Children will be eager to talk when an adult is genuinely interested in what they have to say.

Describe Activities. Playtime or time working in centers provides a great opportunity for you to discuss and describe what the children are doing. Detailing these activities provides you with the chance to use adverbs, adjectives, verbs, and prepositions in a concrete manner, which can enhance language for the children. For example, if a child is playing with play dough, you can say, "Oh, John, I see that you have chosen the yellow and blue play dough. When you roll the play dough together, it begins to turn green."

Use Experiences to Promote New Vocabulary. Introduce new themes, interesting objects, field trips, collections (rocks, small cars, stuffed animals, etc.), books, or classroom visitors that stimulate conversation and encourage children to think, question, and analyze.

ORAL LANGUAGE: DRAMATIC PLAY EXPERIENCES

Dramatic Play Creates Wonderful Conversation and Vocabulary Building Opportunities

Play provides opportunities to use language in new ways. You can suggest songs, plays, show-and-tell, and dramatic play experiences that can incorporate fun, new vocabulary. For example, if children in the dramatic play area are pretending to be working at a hospital, you can introduce specific vocabulary words such as *emergency, temperature, thermometer, first aid, bandages, wound,* etc.

Dramatic play builds oral language through the following ways:

♦ encouraging children to learn words that they might not use in everyday situations;

♦ aiding in the development of children's social skills and social vocabulary;

♦ helping children learn to listen to each other;

♦ facilitating the taking of turns in play and in conversation;

♦ encouraging shy or hesitant children to speak up is easier when they are pretending to be someone else;

♦ modeling new vocabulary, which provides children an opportunity to use language they will need someday in the real world.

Create Dramatic Play Centers and Remember . . .

Dress-up clothes: Ask parents to contribute old clothing including hats, purses, jewelry, Halloween and party costumes, shoes, scarves, and fabric. Think about well-loved storybook characters and try to add items that these characters might need, such as a crown for a princess, a cape for a superhero, or a badge for a police officer.

Props: Each dramatic play center should have appropriate props. For example, a pet shop would need stuffed or plastic animals, a cash register, money, shopping bags, empty (and clean) pet food containers, animal beds and toys, grooming tools, etc. The more props you provide, the longer and more imaginative the play will be.

Children's ideas for dramatic play: Find out the children's special interests and create play centers for those interests. For example, many children love dinosaurs. Set up an archeological dig site with tools, plastic dinosaurs, bones, bowls for washing and cleaning bones, and books and posters about dinosaurs. After the dig, children could create a museum display.

Spontaneous dramatic play opportunities: Look for opportunities to encourage dramatic play whenever the children are playing. For example, when children are playing in the sandbox or classroom with small vehicles, you might say, "Oh, do your cars need any gas?" Then, help the children come up with ways to create a pretend service station.

Integrated Language and Vocabulary Learning

Children learn vocabulary best when it is presented in a meaningful context. Encourage vocabulary development throughout the entire day and in all the content areas: math, social studies, science, literacy, art, physical education, and music. Daily academic learning and repeated exposure to new concepts and ideas will greatly help children learn the new, corresponding vocabulary words.

ORAL LANGUAGE: VOCABULARY BUILDING ACTIVITIES

Robust Vocabulary Instruction—Three "Tiers" of Words

Vocabulary should be carefully chosen and explicitly taught. It is recommended that teachers choose new words based on the stories or rhymes the children are listening to or the unfamiliar words they will encounter through the experiences of a new thematic instructional unit. Words can also be chosen according to three different "tiers." Because not all words have equal importance in language instruction, there is a system that divides words into three levels and helps teachers choose what words to teach (Beck, McKeown, and Kucan 2002).

Tier One—Basic Vocabulary

Tier one words rarely require direct instruction. They are common words that children seem to naturally learn, such as: *book, girl, boy, happy, sad, go, eat, run, dog*, and *toy*. These words are generally nouns, verbs, and adjectives.

Tier Two—High-Frequency, Multiple-Meaning Vocabulary

Tier two represents a more sophisticated vocabulary. These new words are not common to young children's oral language. However, tier two words appear frequently in stories and are words for which children may already have conceptual understanding. They are usually interesting words that can be explained easily so that young children will understand their meanings.

Examples of tier two words are: *commotion, reluctant, fortunate, measure*, and *sincere*. This vocabulary is often descriptive and rich and adds to the content of the text.

Tier Three—Low-Frequency, Content-Specific Vocabulary

Tier three consists of rare words that occur in specific contexts or domains. These low-frequency words are usually learned when the need arises, such as when listening to a passage about ants. Specific words unknown to a child may include: *thorax, compound eye, abdomen, antennae, mandibles*, and *tibial spur*.

Sorting Activities Strengthen Vocabulary

Sorting objects by concept gives children the opportunity to compare and contrast, which provides vocabulary building experiences. First, provide a predetermined sort, such as sorting furniture and clothing. For this sort, children need to discern how the object is used in order to be able to place it in the correct category. There are many other ways that children can sort objects, such as by shape, color, texture, or size.

Build Vocabulary Using Photographs

Collect a large assortment of photographs and use them in a variety of ways to build vocabulary. Glue them to index cards for matching games and concentration. Display photos on bulletin boards according to themes for children to look at and discuss. Create photo albums of topics children are especially interested in. Make classification games using photographs. Photograph the children's daily activities, place the photos in a classroom album, and add to it through the year. (This will become a classroom favorite.)

Box of Puppets

Collect puppets and keep them in the dramatic play area. Children who are shy often find additional confidence while holding a puppet as they speak. Use animal puppets when retelling animal stories.

Story Boxes

Select some of your favorite children's books and create a story box for each book. Add things from the story that the children can use to help them retell the tale or create new scenarios for the story.

ORAL LANGUAGE: SHARED READING

What Is Shared Reading?

Shared reading, developed by Don Holdaway in 1979, is an interactive reading experience where children join in the reading of a big book or other enlarged text as guided by an adult. Unlike simply being read to, children interact with the text during shared reading. It is through shared reading that the adult demonstrates the reading process and reading strategies. Shared reading also provides excellent opportunities to explain concepts about print and features of books. The books chosen for shared reading should be engaging texts that will be enjoyed for multiple readings.

During shared reading, students are learning to do the following:

- track print from left to right and word by word and return sweep;
- find letters and sounds in context;
- predict, infer, and draw conclusions;
- enjoy and participate in reading with a high level of support;
- build a sense of story;
- expand vocabulary;
- point out concepts of print (spacing, capitalization, punctuation, etc.);
- sequence the events of a story;
- focus on story elements (characters, setting, beginning, middle, end, etc.).

The Shared Reading Experience

1. **Gather the children so that they all can see.** The children should be seated in a comfortable area. Place the book on a chart or easel so that the children can easily see the pictures and text. You may wish to use a pointer to guide the reading. During shared reading, students focus on both the pictures and the text.

2. **Introduce the book.** Show the book to the children. Share the theme and discuss the title, cover, and cover illustrations. Ask the students to predict what they think the story will be about. Encourage them to use previous or background knowledge. Get the students excited about the upcoming story!

3. **Read the story for the first time.** Read the book to students and check their predictions against the text of the story. (At this point, you are almost entirely responsible for the reading of the text.) Concentrate on enjoying the story and read it through with only a few stops. Although you are reading the whole story, students should still be encouraged to spontaneously participate in its reading and discuss personal responses to it. ALWAYS be positive in acknowledging children's responses.

4. **Continue with subsequent readings and follow-up activities.** Revisit the book for several days. The children's comprehension of the story will increase through questioning and story discussion. Talk about the author's choice of words and the illustrator's pictures. Once students are familiar with the story, look more closely at the text itself. The children's participation may range from reading out loud to silently mouthing a few of the words. Use the following strategies to increase reading behaviors, comprehension, and vocabulary development:

   - perform choral readings
   - act out the story
   - sort words into categories
   - mask certain letters
   - record children reading the text
   - sequence the events of the story
   - facilitate word work, such as "Be the Words"
   - hunt for high-frequency words
   - use oral cloze (while choral reading, pause or drop your voice out completely)
   - focus on sounds, rhyming words, or words that begin with the same sound
   - review story elements, such as setting, characters, problem, or solution
   - make a classroom big book in response to the shared reading book experience

ORAL LANGUAGE: DIALOGIC READING

A Great Combination—Dialogic Reading and Shared Reading

Dialogic reading (from the word *dialogue*) is an intervention strategy based on the work of Dr. Grover Whitehurst and the Stony Brook Reading and Language Project. As Dr. Whitehurst states, "In dialogic reading, the adult helps the child become the teller of the story. The adult becomes the listener, the questioner, the audience for the child. . . . Children learn most from books when they are actively involved." (Whitehurst 1992) Virtually all children's books are appropriate for dialogic reading. The best books have detailed illustrations. Use the child's interests as your guide for choosing books.

Whitehurst outlines the fundamental reading technique in dialogic reading as the **PEER** sequence. This is a short interaction between a child and an adult.

The adult

Prompts the child to say something about the book

Evaluates the child's response

Expands the child's response by rephrasing and adding information

Repeats the prompt to assess what the child has learned and understands

---

For example, the adult and the child are looking at the page of a book that has a picture of a farmyard scene. The adult says, (the **P**rompt) "What is the chicken doing?" while pointing to the chicken. The child says, (the **E**valuation) "Running around." The adult continues, (**E**valuation and **E**xpansion) "Yes, the chicken is running around by the fence. (**R**epeat prompt) What is the chicken doing?" The child responds, "The chicken is running around in circles by the fence."

After you have first shared a book with a child, initiate a **PEER** sequence on almost every page for subsequent readings. You may read the written words on a page, and then encourage the child to say something in response. As you reread the book together, read fewer of the words each time, allowing the child to do more.

Five types of prompts are used in dialogic reading to begin **PEER** sequences. Use the acronym **CROWD** to remember the five prompts.

Completion prompts: Pause at the end of a sentence and allow the child to fill in the blank. These completion prompts are most often used in books with repetitive phrases or rhymes, for example, "Jack and Jill went up the _____."

Recall prompts: Asking the children to talk about what happened in the book helps them remember events in the story and understand the plot.

Open-ended prompts: These prompts focus on a book's illustrations and can help a child focus on details. While looking at a familiar page, you might say, "Tell me about this picture. What do you think the girl is saying?"

Wh-prompts: These prompts ask the questions who, what, when, where, why, and how. *Wh*-prompts are also directed towards the book's illustrations. For example, you might say, "Where is the dog going? How do you think he is feeling?"

Distancing prompts: These prompts help children relate the pictures or words in the book to their own experiences. For example, while looking at a book with a picture of a boat, you might ask, "Have you ever ridden in a boat?"

Dialogic Reading—An Intervention Strategy Found to Be Extremely Successful!

Based on language development tests, children who have been read to dialogically are significantly ahead of children who have been read to traditionally. After just a few weeks of dialogic reading, children can jump ahead by several months. These same results were found with hundreds of children from economic backgrounds ranging from poverty to affluence in areas as geographically different as New York, Tennessee, and Mexico, and in varied settings, such as homes, preschools, and day care centers.

ORAL LANGUAGE: QUESTIONS AND ACTIVITIES FOR BEFORE, DURING, AND AFTER READING

Below are lists of possible questions and activities that can help increase comprehension, vocabulary, thinking skills, decoding skills, and a variety of other early literacy skills. They are intended to be used as springboards. Use them when appropriate.

Questions to ask BEFORE you read:

1. This is the cover of the book. Look at the pictures. What do you think will happen in this book?
2. What makes you think that will happen?
3. Look at the cover. What characters do you think might be in the story?
4. Do you think there will be a problem in this story? Why or why not?
5. Does the story relate to you or your family? How? (This activates background knowledge.)

Activities for BEFORE you read: Review new vocabulary before reading and make a KWL map.

Questions to ask DURING the reading:

1. What has happened so far in the story?
2. What do you think will happen next?
3. How do you think the story will end?
4. How would you have felt if you were that character?
5. Why do you think the character did _____?
6. What would you have done if you were the character?
7. As we read, what were you thinking about?
8. Can you put what we've just read in your own words?
9. Do you like the story so far? Why or why not?
10. Is there anything that you might change in the story?
11. Does this story remind you of another story?

Activities for DURING the reading:

a. Give clues to students who may be stuck or can't remember.
b. Help students use strategies to figure out new words.
c. Help define new vocabulary.

Questions to ask AFTER the reading:

1. Can you remember the title?
2. Was it a good title for this book? Why or why not?
3. Why do you think the author wrote this book?
4. Were your predictions about the story correct?
5. If there was a problem, did it get solved?
6. What happened because of the problem?
7. What was your favorite part of the story?
8. Did you have a favorite character in the story?
9. Is there a character in the story like you? How are you alike?
10. If you could change one thing in the story, what would it be?
11. Can you retell the story in order?
12. If you were _____, how would you have felt?
13. What is the most interesting part of the story?
14. Did you like this book?

Activities for AFTER the reading:

a. Retell all or part of the story.
b. Compare the story to another book.
c. Discuss a new ending for the story.
d. Draw a picture about the story.

Chapter 7
PRINT AWARENESS

The Significance of Print Awareness

Print awareness refers to a child's understanding that print conveys meaning, has different functions, and is organized in a certain way. Print awareness is closely associated with a child's ability to recognize words as separate elements of oral and written communication. Along with phonological awareness, print awareness is a strong determinant of early reading achievement (Adams 1990). Print awareness is a preliteracy skill that children are expected to have mastered by the time they enter first grade.

For many children, this skill is acquired naturally within their home environments. These children are the lucky ones—they come from print-rich homes. These children have parents who have exposed them to many kinds of print and have modeled a wide variety of reasons why and the ways people communicate through reading and writing. Sadly, there are also many children who live in homes with inadequate levels of print and where parents do not frequently model reading and writing. These children will likely begin school at a disadvantage, and, in all probability, will continue to fall behind their peers in literacy achievements.

What Does Print Awareness Include?

Children learn about written language when they have experiences with environmental print, letters, and words. Children must understand the connection that printed words represent spoken words. Following are some ways to assess a child's print awareness:

Book Concepts

- Identifies front and back covers
- Identifies print on a page
- Identifies where one starts reading
- Holds the book right side up
- Turns pages properly and understands page sequence
- Follows text from left to right
- Views pages from top to bottom
- Has developed one-to-one correspondence between oral and written words
- Demonstrates a return sweep
- Understands that words tell a story

Print Concepts

- Is aware of print in the environment
- Understands that print is the words that are read
- Recognizes that words are made up of letters
- Recognizes that there are spaces between words
- Recognizes that sentences are made up of words
- Knows words are read from left to right and from top to bottom
- Understands the difference between pictures and print
- Understands that pictures relate to print
- Observes that print has different functions (street signs, recipes, letters, stories, labels, etc.)

PRINT AWARENESS: ACTIVITIES

Dramatic Play Print

Make sure that you incorporate print into dramatic play themes. For example, add street signs, store names, grocery store packaging, menus, receipts, forms for a doctor's office, magazines, newspapers, letters, or labels. Create print together with your students. Let them practice and play with print.

Make Labels

Use index cards to label (with both words and pictures) objects, toys, and classroom centers. Draw attention to the words when showing the cards to students. Invite children to help make the labels.

Writing Centers

Use ideas from the writing center (page 119). Provide children with the tools to explore the various reasons why we write. Children can pretend to write a shopping list, compose a thank you note, design a birthday card, make a stop sign, draft a letter, create a cereal box, or formulate print for some other product.

Dictation

Take dictation from children. Write their words exactly as they say them while they watch you write the words. Have them touch each word as you read it. Point out that there are spaces between each of the words.

> I like to play.
> Playing is fun.

Story and Rhyme Charts

Large story and rhyme charts are wonderful tools for developing print awareness. Discuss where you should start reading. Touch each word as you read it. Point out that there are spaces between each of the words. Talk about punctuation. Point out that a period tells us that the sentence has ended, and we should pause a moment. Count how many words were in a sentence. Discuss upper- and lowercase letters.

Picture, Letter, Word, and Sentence Sorting

Use commercially made flashcards or create your own. Mix together an assortment of cards that have pictures, individual alphabet letters, single words, and one short sentence per card. Let the children sort the cards and discuss what is on each card.

You can also turn this into a game. Pass out several cards to each child. Say *picture*, *letter*, *word*, or *sentence*. Each time you say a word, if the child has a card of that type, she should run up and give it to you. The first child to have given you all of his cards is the winner!

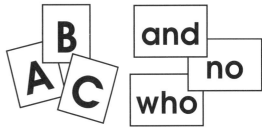

My Own Mailbox

Ask parents to send to school an empty shoe or tissue box. Cover the boxes in white paper and let each child print her name on a box and make a mailbox with a red flag. Let the children have the fun of "writing" and "mailing" letters to each other. Encourage parents to send notes to school for their children that you can put in their mailboxes as a fun surprise.

Environmental Print Matching Fun

Find pictures of a wide variety of environmental print. (These are easy to locate using the Internet.) Choose street signs, stop signs, store signs, billboards, restaurant signs, exit signs, food boxes, or anything that is familiar to the children and something they would recognize. Print two of each picture and glue them to index cards. Use the pairs of cards for matching games such as memory match or concentration.

PRINT AWARENESS: "FOLD-IT" MINI-BOOKS

Four Reproducible "Fold-It" Mini-Books for Print Awareness

Each of the four "Fold-It" Mini-Books provides experiences with specific print and book concepts. They are designed for adults and children to read together. Directions that include guidance questions are printed below. Copy the "Fold-It" Mini-Books and the directions and send both home to children's parents. These will help parents understand how to bring print awareness into their homes and help their children gain early literacy skills.

- ✄

Directions for the "Fold-It" Mini-Books

I Know How to Take Care of Books (page 151)

Concepts: proper care of a book and book etiquette; identifying print on a page

Page 1: Point out the little cat on the cover. She has very clean hands. Read the text. Talk about what would happen if we touched books with dirty hands.

Page 2: Read the text. Ask, "Have you ever scribbled on a book page?" "Would it be fun to read a book that was scribbled all over or cut with scissors?" "How do you think the little cat is feeling about a scribbled page?"

Page 3: Read the text. Talk about how bending pages can hurt a book. Talk about bookmarks. Make a bookmark to use with the next storybook you and the child read together.

Page 4: Read the text. Talk about good places to keep books (e.g., bookshelves, away from water and pets, etc.) Talk about being responsible and taking good care of the stories that your child loves.

Let's Learn about Books (page 152)

Concepts: identifying front and back covers, book title, author, and illustrator; understanding that words tell a story, that pictures relate to print, and the difference between pictures and print; holding a book right side up

Page 1: Point out the little monkey. He is on the front cover of the book. He is pointing to the title of the book. Read the title and touch each word as you read it.

Page 2: Say, "Look at the monkey. The monkey is pointing to the author's name." Talk about what authors do. "Authors write the words in books. The words tell the story." Read the text.

Page 3: Say, "Look, now the monkey is pointing to the illustrator's name." Talk about what illustrators do. "Illustrators create the pictures in books. The pictures help us understand the story." Read the text.

Page 4: This is the back cover of the book. Talk about how we start to read a story in the front of the book, and the story ends in the back of the book. Help the child make his own "Fold-It" Mini-Book. Review each of these concepts as the child makes his own book.

How Should We Read a Book? (page 153)

Concepts: holding a book right side up, viewing a page from top to bottom, following text from left to right, and demonstrating a return sweep; understanding that print is the words we read, sentences are made up of words, there are spaces between words, and words are made up of letters; recognizing one-to-one correspondence between oral and written words

Page 1: Say, "Look at the little owls. One owl is reading the words on this page. Let's read the words with him." Have the child touch each word as you read. Count the words in the sentence. You can also count the words in the title of the book.

Page 2: Read this page. Talk about how we start reading at the top of the page. And, we stop reading at the bottom of the page. Ask the child to point to the first word we would read on this page. Point to the last word on the page.

Page 3: Read this page. Talk about how we read from left to right. Read the sentence and have the child touch each word and move her finger from left to right as you read. Count how many words are in the sentence. Talk about the spaces between the words. Point to one letter and then point to a word.

Page 4: Read this page. Talk about how we read from left to right. Read the sentence and have the child touch each word and move his finger from left to right. Talk about a return sweep. When you get to the right, you SWEEP back to the left and continue reading.

Punctuation! The Stop Signs of a Sentence (page 154)

Concepts: understanding concepts of punctuation (period, question mark, and exclamation mark)

Page 1: Read the title of the book. Ask, "What do you think the words *stop signs of a sentence* mean? Talk about how there are three symbols that tell the reader to stop and give more meaning to the sentence.

Page 2: A period says to stop or pause for a moment. It tell us that the sentence has come to an end.

Page 3: Next is a question mark. It tells us that the sentence is asking something. Take turns asking each other questions so that the child understands what a question is.

Page 4: Now, we see an exclamation mark! It tells us that something is exciting or very important.

FOLD #1

I use a bookmark. I never bend the pages.

-3-

I never write, draw, or color on or cut or glue the pages of a book.

-2-

-4-

I keep my books safe.
I keep them away from water,
pets, paint, mud, and babies!

-1-

A "Fold-It" Mini-Book

I Know How to Take Care of Books

Look! I have clean hands!
I only touch books with
clean hands!

FOLD #2

This is the illustrator's name.
The illustrator draws the pictures
for the book. The pictures help us
understand the story.

This is the author's name.
The author writes the
words for the book.
The words tell us the story.

FOLD #1

-3-

-2-

-4-

-1-

This is the back cover of the book.

The story is at THE END!

FOLD #2

Let's Learn about Books

by
Sherrill B. Flora

Illustrations by
Julie Anderson

This is the front cover of the book.

This is the title.

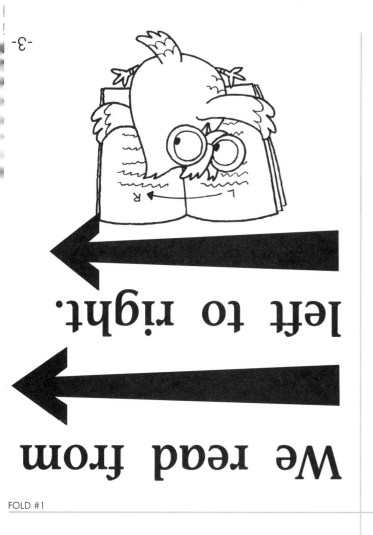

We read from left to right.

FOLD #1

We read from the top to the bottom of the page.

This is the last page.

The End

A "Fold-It" Mini-Book

How Should We Read a Book?

Books have words.

FOLD #2

A question mark is put at
the end of a sentence.
A sentence with a question mark
asks a question.

FOLD #1

-3-

A period is put at
the end of a sentence.
A sentence with a period
tells us something.

-2-

-4-

An exclamation mark is put at
the end of a sentence.
An exclamation mark tells us
something is exciting or important.

FOLD #2

-1-

A "Fold-It" Mini-Book

Punctuation!
The Stop Signs of a Sentence

Chapter 8

TIPS TO ASSIST PARENT INVOLVEMENT

What Recent Research Has to Say about Parent Involvement

Decades of research show that children will experience more school success when their parents are involved. Here are some statistical facts:

◆ Family participation in education was twice as predictive of students' academic success as family socioeconomic status. Some of the more intensive programs had effects that were 10 times greater than other factors.

◆ When schools encourage children to practice reading at home with parents, the children make significant gains in reading achievement compared to those who only practice at school.

◆ The more intensely parents are involved, the more beneficial the achievement effects.

◆ Parents, who read to their children, have books available, take trips, guide TV watching, and provide stimulating experiences contribute to student achievement.

Years of research show that parental involvement with their children's education results in:

◆ Higher grades, test scores, and graduation rates

◆ Better school attendance

◆ Increased motivation, better self-esteem

◆ Lower rates of suspension

Share Ideas and Information with Parents

Teachers can share with parents many suggestions that will help them assist their children in acquiring the skills necessary for becoming good readers.

◆ **Sharing information informally.** Share with the families the value of language play in the home. This can be done at informal times such as when parents drop off and pick up their children at school. The school can also send home newsletters and other forms of communication that will give parents information about encouraging early literacy skills.

◆ **Schedule home visits.** When possible, schedule home visits with each family. These give parents an opportunity to get to know you as well as you getting to know them, and better understand the child's home environment.

◆ **Invite parents to visit the classroom.** Encourage parents to come to school with their child and stay to observe what is going on in the classroom. This will help parents understand new terms such as *phonological awareness* and *print concepts*. The more parents understand early literacy practices, the more they will be able to help their children.

◆ **Demonstrate early literacy ideas.** Invite parents to attend a read aloud story time. Demonstrate how to model language skills, play with language, point out new vocabulary, etc. Observing a teacher reading aloud will give parents lots of knowledge that will help them read to their own children.

◆ **Send home the reproducible parent tip sheets (Pages 156–160).** On the following pages you will find Parent Tip Sheets that can be reproduced and sent home. Use the topics as they blend in with your own curriculum. Encourage parents to post these tips on the refrigerator so that they can keep them in view.

◆ **Share the reproducible bookmark (Page 160).** Send many of these bookmarks home with the children. Include a note explaining that each time the parent and child read a story together, the parent should write the title on the bookmark, and the child should draw a small picture of part of the story or of a favorite character.

Create a Love of Reading That Will Last a Lifetime!

- Read often to your child and have fun.
- Snuggle together when you read.
- Read and reread and reread the stories that your child loves.
- Make predictions (let your child tell what he thinks will happen next).
- Enjoy and talk about the illustrations.
- Talk about the authors and illustrators of the books you read.
- Listen to books on tape.
- Have your child read into a tape recorder once a month and share the progress with her.
- Read aloud together with your child.
- Leave out a word or phrase on each page. For example, say, "Little Red Riding Hood said, 'Oh, what big _____ you have, Grandma!'")

- Have your child think of a new ending to the story.
- When reading a nonfiction book, ask your child what he know about the topic and what he wants to learn.
- When you read, involve your child by having her point out objects in the pictures and follow the words with her finger.
- Read poems with your child.
- Read children's magazines together.
- Try echo reading. Choose something fun to read, such as a poem, song, or joke. Read a sentence with expression and then ask your child to repeat the sentence after you.
- Check out the public library.
- Create a special place in your home for your child's books.
- Keep a few "old favorite" books in the car to enjoy.

LIST OF GREAT READ-ALOUD BOOKS

Animals Should Definitely Not Wear Clothing. Judi Barrett. (Atheneum, 1970)

Anno's Counting House. Mitsumasa Anno. (Philomel Books, 1982)

Bearsie Bear and the Surprise Sleepover Party. Bernard Waber. (Houghton Mifflin, 1997)

Blueberries for Sal. Robert McCloskey. (Viking Books, 1976)

Brown Bear, Brown Bear, What Do You See? Bill Martin Jr. (Henry Holt and Co., 1996)

Bunny Cakes. Rosemary Wells. (Puffin Books, 2000)

Chicka Chicka Boom Boom. Bill Martin Jr. (Beach Lane Books, 2009)

Dinorella: A Prehistoric Fairy Tale. Pamela Duncan Edwards. (Hyperion, 1997)

Elmer. David McKee. (HarperCollins, 1989)

The Enormous Crocodile. Roald Dahl. (Knopf Books, 2000)

First Day Jitters. Julie Danneberg. (Charlesbridge Publishing, 2000)

Flossie and the Fox. Patricia McKissack. (Dutton Books, 1986)

The Foot Book. Dr. Seuss. (Random House, 1968)

Good Driving, Amelia Bedelia. Peggy Parish. (HarperTrophy, 1996)

Goodnight Moon. Margaret Wise Brown. (HarperCollins, 1976)

Green Eggs and Ham. Dr. Seuss. (Random House, 1968)

Growing Vegetable Soup. Lois Ehlert. (Harcourt, 1987)

Hello, Mrs. Piggle-Wiggle. Betty MacDonald. (HarperCollins, 1957)

Hop on Pop. Dr. Seuss. (Random House, 1976)

Horace. Holly Keller. (Greenwillow, 1991)

I Know an Old Lady Who Swallowed a Fly. Simms Taback. (Viking, 1997)

If You Give a Moose a Muffin. Laura Numeroff. (Laura Geringer, 1991)

James and the Giant Peach. Roald Dahl. (Puffin, 2000)

The Little Engine That Could. Watty Piper. (Grosset & Dunlap, 1978)

Little Red Riding Hood: A Newfangled Prairie Tale. Lisa Campbell Ernst. (Simon & Schuster, 1995)

Madeline. Ludwig Bemelmans. (Viking, 1958)

Make Way for Ducklings. Robert McCloskey. (Viking, 1941)

Millions of Cats. Wanda Gág. (Rebound by Sagebrush, 1999)

Miss Rumphius. Barbara Cooney. (Viking, 1982)

The Mitten. Jan Brett. (Putnam Juvenile, 1989)

The Mixed-Up Chameleon. Eric Carle. (HarperTrophy, 1988)

My Very First Mother Goose. Iona Opie. (Candlewick, 1999)

Nana Upstairs, Nana Downstairs. Tomie De Paola. (Putnam, 1975)

The Napping House. Audrey and Don Wood. (Harcourt, 1984)

The New Adventures of Mother Goose. Bruce Lansky. (Meadowbrook, 1993)

Olivia. Ian Falconer. (Atheneum, 2000)

One Fish, Two Fish, Red Fish, Blue Fish. Dr. Seuss. (Random House, 1976)

The Polar Express. Chris Van Allsburg. (Houghton Mifflin, 1985)

The Red Balloon. Albert Lamorisse. (Doubleday, 1967)

The Snowy Day. Ezra Jack Keats. (Viking, 1962)

The Story of Babar. Jean de Brunhof. (Random House, 1937)

The Story of Ferdinand. Munro Leaf. (Viking, 1936)

Swimmy. Leo Lionni. (Knopf Books, 1992)

The Three Little Pigs. James Marshall. (Puffin Books, 1996)

Town Mouse, Country Mouse. Jan Brett. (Putnam, 1994)

Why Mosquitoes Buzz in People's Ears. Verna Aardema. (Dial, 1975)

The 20th Century Children's Book Treasury: Picture Books and Stories to Read Aloud. Janet Schulman. (Knopf, 1998)

BUILDING ALPHABET KNOWLEDGE

Letters Everywhere!

Point out letters in the environment, on billboards, street signs, store signs, or on food cartons.

Cut and Paste Letters and Names

Children love learning how to read and spell their names. Look through old magazines and cut out the letters that spell your child's name. Glue them in order on a sheet of paper. Also, look for and cut out all of the uppercase letters of the alphabet and glue them in order on a piece of paper.

Alphabet Books

Read alphabet books with your child. Here are three favorite titles:

Chicka Chicka Boom Boom by Bill Martin Jr. and John Archambault (Beach Lane Books, 2009)

Eating the Alphabet: Fruits & Vegetables from A to Z by Lois Ehlert (Harcourt, 1996)

Dr. Seuss's ABC: An Amazing Alphabet Book! by Theodor Geisel (Random House, 1996)

Look Alike Letters

Look through a favorite children's book and go on a letter hunt. If you are reading a Curious George book, maybe it would be fun to look for all the Cs (for *curious*), Gs (for *George*), or even Ms (for *monkey*).

Magnetic Letters

Place a set of magnetic letters on the lower part of your refrigerator. Your child will have hours of fun playing with the letters. Show your child how to spell the names of family members with them.

Alphabet Cereal

Let your child have the fun of finding and matching letters that are the same using alphabet-shaped cereal.

Letter Lineup

Make two sets of alphabet cards. Let your child lay them out in alphabetical order as you sing the "Alphabet Song." The cards can also be used to play a memory match game. Use only four to seven letters at first for the game, so that your child will feel more successful.

ENCOURAGING ORAL LANGUAGE

Tell a Family History Story

Telling stories and reading aloud to your child builds oral language skills. Your child will love hearing you tell stories about your childhood. Encourage your child to ask questions about your childhood and the things that you liked to do when you were little. Ask your child to tell you a story about his own childhood. Listen to your child and let him practice speaking and using new words.

Read Pictures

Look at books or magazines with your child. Encourage your child to look at the details in a picture. Ask your child questions about the pictures that will encourage her to use new words. For example ask, "Which car is larger? Why do you think the man is laughing?" Make up stories about the pictures you are looking at.

Take "Talk Walks" Together

Walking together provides wonderful opportunities for sharing thoughts and stories and for increasing your child's observational skills. Talk about the things you see and encourage new vocabulary. For example say, "Look at that nest in the tree. How do you think the birds built that nest? What materials did they use to build it? Do you think birds hibernate or do they migrate?" Talk about hibernation and migration. The child will learn a lot about new things and will build her vocabulary.

Share Rhyming Stories & Nursery Rhymes

Read some nursery rhymes or rhyming stories with your child. After your child is familiar with the rhyme, stop at the end of a phrase and let him fill in the missing word. For example say, "Jack and Jill went up the ___. When your child begins to understand rhyming, create new rhymes from the traditional nursery rhymes, such as, Jack and Jill had a friend named *Bill*.

Act Out a Favorite Story

Let your child retell a favorite story using small dolls or puppets as the characters. This dramatization is wonderful for building language skills and for helping children recall story details.

Parent Tip Sheet

PHONEMIC AWARENESS

What Is Phonemic Awareness?

It is the understanding that speech is made up of a series of individual sounds (called phonemes). It is the ability to hear these individual sounds in words and the ability to manipulate the sounds in words orally.

Support phonemic awareness by:

- reading nursery rhymes and singing songs
- playing rhyming games
- playing with magnetic letters
- clapping and tapping to demonstrate patterns in songs, stories, and words
- separating words into individual sounds
- participating in word play where children change beginning, middle, and ending sounds

As your child is ready:

- blend letters when learning common spelling and sound patterns
- decode big words by decoding smaller words or word parts within them

Play Phonemic Awareness Games with Your Child

Below you will find a "developmental" list of activities to reinforce what is happening in your child's classroom.

These activities are intended to be done orally for short periods of time—about 5 to 10 minutes daily. This should be fun and not work. Play these games with your child when driving in the car, while taking a bath, or any time during the day. All of these games will help your child develop the skills for learning how to read.

Rhyming Awareness

Read and teach your child nursery rhymes. Substitute rhyming words in the rhymes such as: Hickory, dickory, *dock*. The mouse ran up the *clock*. Change the word *clock* to another rhyming word such as *sock*, *block*, or *rock*.

Read Dr. Seuss books, which are excellent for listening to and discovering fun words that rhyme and for making up new rhyming words.

Word and Syllable Awareness

Teach your child how to clap out syllables, such as *puppy*. Your child should say, "pup–py" and clap twice—one time for each syllable. The following are some multisyllable words to try:

two syllable words:

playground	sandbox	crayons	monkey
baseball	dollhouse	rainbow	snowman

three syllable words:

elephant	dinosaur	telephone	Saturday
camera	September	department	family

four syllable words:

caterpillar	watermelon	harmonica	elevator
celebration	alligator	January	helicopter

Begin with two-syllable words and increase the difficulty level by using words with three- and four-syllable words as your child is ready.

Word Family Awareness

Use the word family chart below. Say a word while stretching out the sounds, such as "C....at. Then, ask your child, "What is the word?" *(cat)* Continue with the same word family to reinforce rhyming, vowel patterns, and sound blending.

Word Families:

–at	–an	–it	–en	–ot	–ake	–ane	–ole
cat	ran	bit	hen	dot	cake	plane	sole
sat	fan	hit	pen	cot	sake	cane	whole
bat	man	sit	ten	tot	rake	lane	mole
fat	can	fit	men	lot	make	mane	pole

Consonants, Vowels & Word Families

Consonants

b	c	d	f	g	h	j	k	l	m
n	p	q	r	s	t	v	w	x	y	z

Vowels

a   e   i   o   u   sometimes y

Short Vowel Sounds

a	e	i	o	u
cat	pen	it	top	cup

Long Vowels Sounds (They say own names.)

"a"	"e"	"i"	"o"	"u"
cake	me	tie	no	cute
say	meet	wife	poke	hue
train	eat	night	boat	cue

The 36 Most Common Word Families

–ack	–ain	–ake	–ale	–all	–ame
–an	–ank	–ap	–ash	–at	–ate
–aw	–ay	–eat	–ell	–est	–ice
–ick	–ide	–ight	–ill	–in	–ine
–ing	–ink	–ip	–ir	–ock	–oke
–op	–or	–ore	–uck	–ug	–ump

WHAT IS INVENTED SPELLING?

Parents of beginning writers often look at their children's sentences and see something like this: We wnt tu sool toode. Translation: "We went to school today."

Often, when children are first learning how to write, they use what is called **"invented spelling."** This means that children listen to the sounds they think they hear in words and write down the letters that they think make those sounds.

Invented spelling is an important stage in your child's learning how to write. In late kindergarten and early first grade, young children are still learning and practicing which letters make which sounds. **Invented spelling is a great way for children to practice which sounds go with which letter!**

Help your child learn to "stretch out" the words she is trying to spell. Saying a word while stretching out the sounds will help the child hear all of the sounds in the word. For example, cat should be stretched out into three sounds, c . . . a . . .t. **Have your child say the word slowly and listen to all of the sounds.**

Although invented spelling is often wrong, do not correct your child. Young children need to feel as if they are being successful. This will encourage them to want to write more.

Ask your child to read what they wrote. Chances are you will not be able to read it yet. It is important for your child to be able to read her writing.

Invented spelling—how children most often begin:

◆ Children first write using beginning sounds. For example, a "d" written for the word *dog*.

◆ **Next, the child will write words using beginning and ending sounds.** So, the word *dog* might now be written as *dg*.

◆ Eventually, usually in first grade, the child will begin to add the middle sounds and will write the word *dog* correctly.

Continually encourage your child to write and draw pictures. This will help create a love of writing. **And, don't worry; eventually your child will be able to spell words accurately.**

EARLY WRITING EXPERIENCES

Drawing Pictures

Drawing and scribbling are often the first steps towards learning how to write. Encourage your child to draw pictures and then ask him to tell you all about his picture. Ask specific questions, such as, "I see you drew a dog. What is the dog's name? What is he doing? What kinds of things do you think this dog would like to do?"

Signing Your Name

Often, one of the first words a child wants to write is her name. Help your child learn how to form the letters of her name. Encourage your child to sign her name on her artwork. Let her sign her name on cards and letters to friends and family.

Why Write?

Children need to understand that writing has a purpose. Let your child see you writing and help you write things for specific reasons. For example, have your child help you write a shopping list, a reminder note, a thank you note, or the address on an envelope.

Lots of Writing Materials

Have a special place in your home where your child can go to find paper, pencils, crayons, pens, markers, a small chalkboard, and chalk. Your child will enjoy practicing writing when she has the necessary materials available to her.

A Book about Me

Work together to make a book. On the first page have your child draw a picture of himself and label it. Next, draw family members, pets, favorite toys, or favorite activities. If your child is very young, have him dictate a sentence about the picture. An older child may want to try and write his own words. Remember to praise all efforts!

Write Letters to Family

Encourage your child to write notes to family. These can be pictures, birthday cards, or thank you notes. Encourage family members to write back to your child. This will help your child understand that writing is another form of communication.

Teach Your Child to Love Books!

One of the best ways to help your child want to become a "reader" is by giving him reasons and lots of opportunities to read. Go to the library often and let your child explore all of the different kinds of books, magazines, and audio materials. Talk about your child's special interests and find books that motivate those interests.

When Reading Together Discuss the Following:

- **Introduce the book.** Read the title, and then the author's and illustrator's names. Study the cover. Ask if the cover gives any clues about what the book might be about. Talk about things your child should listen for.

- **Run your finger under the text while reading.** This teaches your child that people read from left to right and from the top of the page to the bottom.

- **Ask and answer questions** as you read the story together.

- **Talk about the story** during and after reading.

- **Use information and reference books** to answer child's questions if needed.

- **Ask your child to look closely at the pictures.** Help your child learn that pictures can give clues that will help her understand the story.

- **Make predictions.** Ask your child what she thinks might happen next. Or, ask her how a character might be feeling.

- **Repeat interesting words and rhymes.** Explain the meanings of new words.

- **Teach repetitive or predictable phrases.** Your child will love to be able to recite these types of phrases as you read.

- **Ask thinking questions.** "What might happen next? Where did she go? Why did he do that? How do you think she is feeling?"

- **Story Follow-Up Activities.** Plan an activity to extend the story, such as drawing a picture about the story, making a food from the story, learning more about an animal that was in the story.

Other Things to Point Out While Reading Together:

- Talk about specific letters.

- Point out special words.

- Show your child the first word of a sentence.

- Show your child the last word of a sentence.

- Point out the first and last words on a page.

- Discuss punctuation marks and what they mean.

- Point out capital letters. Tell your child that a sentence always begin with a capital letter.

- Ask your child to show you a lowercase letter.

We read the book:

Print title

Draw a picture about the story.